INTRODUCTION: Hiking in Yosemite

The ten trail trips described here are not just happy hikes for visitors who would rather walk than ride, although they are that, too. They are chosen to portray the park story — the renowned Yosemite Valley of waterfalls and domes, the groves of world-giant sequoia trees, and the glaciated High Sierra wilderness. They lead over granite, below waterfalls, through forests, and past wildflower meadows to alpine lakes and mountain summits. The trips range from less-than-a-day walks to 3-day or more backpacks, and a ski tour.

John Muir was perhaps the greatest Yosemite hiker, and you might enjoy carrying along a copy of Muir's *The Yosemite* to read on the trail. His writings, inspired by the Yosemite scene of over 100 years ago, now in turn inspire another generation to enjoy that scene, too, and to keep it intact. Some even call him the father of the park.

It is fitting that the John Muir trail begins in Yosemite Valley, passing through Little Yosemite, Tuolumne Meadows, the Lyell Canyon, and many another of Muir's favo-

John Muir

rite late-1800 haunts on its 211-mile way through the High Sierra to Mount Whitney.

On your trips, also take along a pocket magnifier and a binocular to extend your scope of vision in both directions of focus — from the minutiae of flower parts and rock crystals to antics of animals too wary for approach or to cleavage details of peaks too distant to climb. Many hikers carry cameras, too.

To the hiker, Yosemite National Park is a 1,189 square-mile wildland laced with over 750 miles of trails. Although large and with remote sections, the park is also accessible for short trips (such as most of those described here): Three year-round roads lead into Yosemite Valley and the uplands on the western side of the park. And in summer the Tioga Road is clear of snow (Memorial Day in late May to November 1 most years), opening the way to the park interior.

You can hike any time in Yosemite. Every season is best. *Spring* in Yosemite Valley is the best place on Earth for waterfalls — with hikes on the flat valley floor mainly, because the high country above will still be closed by snow — the very snow melting over the falls. Above, granite domes billow atop vertical cliff walls. Below, the forested sand flats of filled-in An-

Upper and Lower Yosemite Falls, spring

3

enthusiasts

cient Lake Yosemite remind that the whole is a scene left by Ice Age glaciers.

Summer is best for the mid-altitude forests and meadows. Early, red snowplants emerge in the forest fringe; then in July and even later, white azaleas, orange leopard lilies, and red columbines come out in the wet green meadow centers, making the season seem more like spring. Giant sequoia groves are color in mass: bulbs of rich-green foliage atop tall cinnamon-red pillars thrust high into a sky of azure puffed with clean white cumulous clouds. Higher, streams rush with snowmelt, some hardly having channels to follow they are so very young after the glaciers scoured their beds. At altitudes of 8,000 feet and up the air is rare — enough so that lowland humans notice shortness of breath even with mild exertion. Thus, short trips in and out of the high country can be unpleasant, and you may want to spend your first few days there adjusting before taking more strenuous hikes. You'll often *need* mosquito repellent about 2 to 4 weeks after the snow has melted at any given spot, and you may want it other times also. Thundershowers are frequent during summer afternoons some years and can drench you completely, but generally they clear away soon and end with a drying breeze. Rain is unusual at night, but does occur, so some take tents and some don't. Hikes are more pleasant if begun early enough that steep sections are passed before midday.

Autumn is best for rambling over the wide-open High Sierra granite above timberline. All the last winter's snow is now finally gone, the rock-fringe cassiope has just bloomed after its so-short growing season, and the snow-oriented gray-crowned rosy finch has retreated to the shadows on the north sides of peaks where permanent ice remains the whole year. Except at midday, temperatures are crisp; plant colors are warm yellows, reds, and browns — or deep green on the sparse pines and hemlocks; skies are now ink-blue; and streams are low or dry during this drought time of the year. It's a campfire time of year, too, for nights are long. Hikers, rangers, and deer watch the weather, staying high until the first closing storm of winter and their annual dash downhill. Then it's Yosemite Valley's turn again for best — its oaks, cottonwoods, and willows firing the meadows, riverbanks, and cliffwalls with

atop Lembert Dome in Tuolumne Meadows, summer

TEN TRAIL TRIPS IN YOSEMITE NATIONAL PARK

by William R. Jones
former Chief Park Naturalist

Bill Jones lived and worked in Yosemite National Park for a dozen years and has returned often since to hike its trails, study and teach its geology, and write of its scenic wonders. He has a degree in geology from Stanford University and has experience in that field as well as those of park ranger, park naturalist, interpretive planner, and park planner. He is author of several popular books and articles on the park, and has more in preparation.

Contents

	Page
INTRODUCTION: Hiking in Yosemite	3
1) YOSEMITE VALLEY FLOOR / Lower Yosemite Fall to Mirror Lake	9
2) YOSEMITE VALLEY WALL / Glacier Point to Yosemite Valley Floor	17
3) WATERFALLS AND DOMES / Vernal-Nevada Falls, with Half Dome option	22
4) GIANT SEQUOIAS / Mariposa Grove	30
5) HIGH SIERRA / May Lake and Mount Hoffman	42
6) GLACIAL LANDSCAPE / Tuolumne Meadows-Lembert Dome	49
7) YOSEMITE WILDERNESS / Tuolumne River to Waterwheel Falls	54
8) SIERRA CREST / Mount Dana	58
9) LIVING GLACIERS / Lyell and Maclure	64
10) WINTER / Ostrander Hut Ski Trail	72

Although this guide combines long experience of persons on the National Park Service ranger and naturalist staffs at Yosemite both now and in the past, conditions do change. Never rely completely on the printed word, maps, signs, or even verbal instructions, but rather temper all with your own judgment. After all, part of going into the wilderness is to accept the responsibility of self-reliance it not only connotes but sometimes requires.

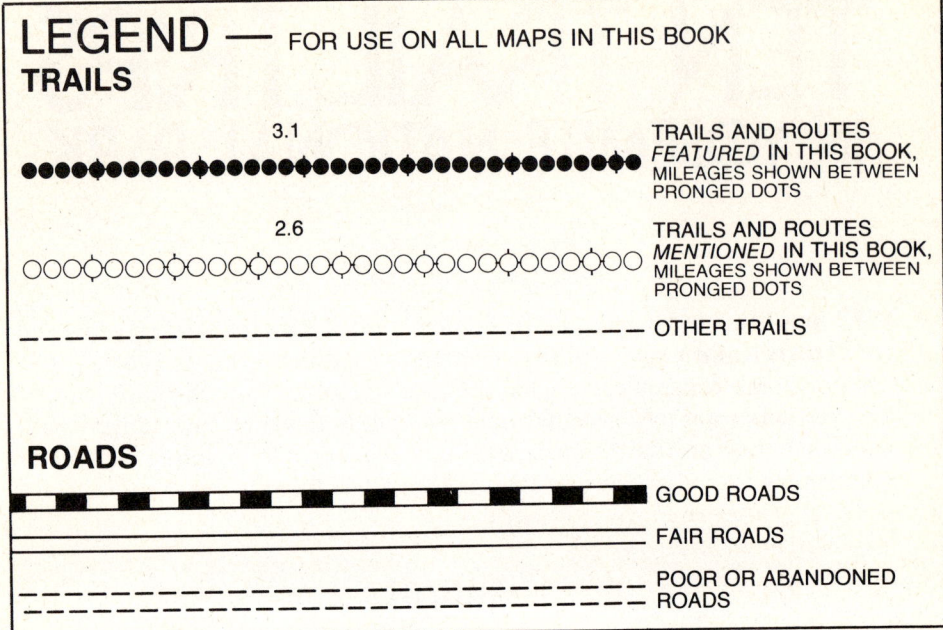

ACKNOWLEDGEMENTS: Most of the maps are copies of those published by the United States Geological Survey, with trail emphasis added by Gary Hurelle. The drawing of Yosemite Valley was furnished by the Denver Service Center of the National Park Service. Mileages were provided by the engineering and maintenance division of Yosemite National Park and many photographs were furnished by the park's superintendent and interpretive offices. For many of the balance, Russell Jones gets much of the credit for carrying the heavy camera up steep trails. Naturalist and ranger personnel at Yosemite who helped read the text include John Krisko (District Naturalist, Tuolumne Meadows), Ron Mackie (Backcountry Unit Manager), and Bill Wendt (Chief Park Ranger). Warren White helped with the ski trails. Comments were also solicited from Henry Berrey of the Yosemite Natural History Association and John Graham of the Yosemite Park and Curry Co. Dear Yosemite friends — the Rusts, Saulsburys, Davisons, and many more — gave much appreciated hospitality in the park during the field work.

COPYRIGHT © 1977, 1981

a publishing and distributing company since 1972

OUTBOOKS
217 Kimball Ave.
Golden, CO 80401

Revised and updated 1981

ISBN 0-89646-064-9

their brilliance, inviting strolls and even more ambitious hikes now that the heat is gone.

Winter is best, too, with virtually all the park an untrammeled wilderness once more after every snowstorm — perfect for skiers and snowshoers. Or it may be a hiking time, at least in lower areas like the floor of Yosemite Valley, snows vary so much from year to year.

While most trails included here are maintained by park crews and are easy to follow, some are not, and still others are cross-country trips and scrambles or include optional but bonafide mountain climbs. Several — especially on side trips — are identified as mere "use trails" where repeated walking has worn a path, sometimes barely discernible. So, avoid potential problems by staying within the limits of your experience and ability. Leave an itinerary with friend or family. Know that trails ascending the valley walls were historically located for summer, not winter, use, and most have severe hazards from falling ice and snow during much of most winters and well into the spring months. The same is true in many backcountry areas, even though not always mentioned in this text.

Watch for simple hazards, too. Loose sand grains on a steep trail surface act like ball-bearings when stepped on. Shoes with non-skid soles are essential for most Yosemite hikes. Even moderately-pitched granite slabs are too slick to stand on where smooth, polished, or wet. Place your steps on them carefully, watching for rough spots and little ledges to hold you, or stay off entirely. A brimmed hat and sunglasses enhance comfort on the many bright days, and can be near-vital at high altitudes or after snows. Sunburn preventative is often necessary. Consider taking flashlight, parka, water, food, and first-aid kit.

Some trails serve both hikers and horseback riders; horses do have the right-of-way and where terrain permits hikers must move off the trail and then stand quietly and still so as not to frighten the passing horses and endanger their riders.

Topographic maps are included for each

winter in the backcountry

western juniper and Tenaya Lake

trip, reproduced from those published by the U.S. Geological Survey and so based on the best available data from aerial photographs. Most hikers today know how these maps show all three dimensions, but they may not realize their limitations. For instance, the maps cannot show any relief feature smaller than the contour interval. Thus a 60-foot tall rock spire prominent in your view may not even show on a map with an 80-foot contour interval. Worse, a 10-foot band of cliff across an otherwise negotiable rock slope could completely block your way but would not show. Thus, deviations from the routes shown on the maps could prove frustrating or challenging, depending on your mood and your success. Occasionally, locations of trails or other features are either not shown precisely (being hard for the mapmakers to see on the original photos) or have disappeared or been relocated.

Gauge your time. Estimates in this guide are based on a presumed average hiking time of one hour for every two miles of distance, *plus* one hour for every 1,000 feet of elevation gained. Some hikers may need to add an hour for every 1,000 feet of elevation lost, too, while athletic types will find these rules-of-thumb too soft and should substitute their own formulas. Allow extra time for photography, a swim, nature study, fishing, lunch, and layover days on longer trips. On one-day trips, start early enough either to get back before dark or to a safer stretch of trail. Or time your night walk with the calendar for moonlight, picking leveler open areas. Consider taking water on longer hikes (even winter ones), or know where you can find it. And remember that this brief guide can only give general conditions, so check at a ranger station or visitor center for last-minute updates — especially in winter, during spring high water, and for off-trail travel. If you will be out overnight, get a wilderness permit and know what to do about bears so you don't lose your food to them and have to finish your trip hungry and perhaps early. You can find out then, too, about especially interesting seasonal attractions to watch for — lunar rainbows, deer fawning grounds, peak-top polemoniums.

If you would like to help keep the information in these pages as current as possible and therefore useful to future hikers, too, please forward any of your findings to the address on the copyright page. They will be used in making up the next edition. Thanks.

Have a good trip. Or ten!

hiking in the high country

FOR FURTHER INFORMATION

Trail conditions, opening and closing of roads and passes, Ostrander Ski Hut reservations, Wilderness Permits, regulations, park information
- Superintendent, Yosemite National Park, California 95389
- At park headquarters in Yosemite Valley and ranger stations at Wawona, Tuolumne Meadows, etc.

Park topographic maps, trail maps, Yosemite Field Seminars, Yosemite booklets
- Yosemite Natural History Association, Yosemite National Park, California 95389
- At Yosemite Valley Visitor Center and others in park; also at mountaineering centers in Yosemite Valley and Tuolumne Meadows.

Park accommodations, High Sierra Camp reservations
- Yosemite Park & Curry Co., Yosemite National Park, California 95389
- At Yosemite Lodge, Curry Village, and The Ahwahnee in Yosemite Valley; Wawona Hotel at Wawona, Tuolumne Meadows Lodge and White Wolf Lodge.

Mountain photography, park literature
- Ansel Adams Gallery, Yosemite National Park, California 95389
- In Yosemite Valley at Yosemite Village.

Free hiking and outdoor books catalog (issued intermittently; dealer inquiries invited)
- Outbooks, 217 Kimball Ave., Golden, Colorado 80401

Yosemite Valley,
showing featured trails

1. Bridalveil Fall
2. Cathedral Rocks
3. Cathedral Spires
4. El Capitan
5. Glacier Point
6. Half Dome
7. Illilouette Fall
8. Lost Arrow
9. Mirror Lake
10. Nevada Fall
11. Ribbon Fall
12. Royal Arches
13. Sentinel Dome
14. Sentinel Rock
15. Three Brothers
16. Vernal Fall
17. Washington Column
18. Yosemite Fall
19. Ahwahnee Hotel
20. Campgrounds
21. Curry Village
22. Employee Housing and Maintenance
23. Happy Isles
24. Housekeeping Camp
25. Pines Campgrounds
26. Sunnyside Campground
27. Village Mall
28. Yosemite Lodge

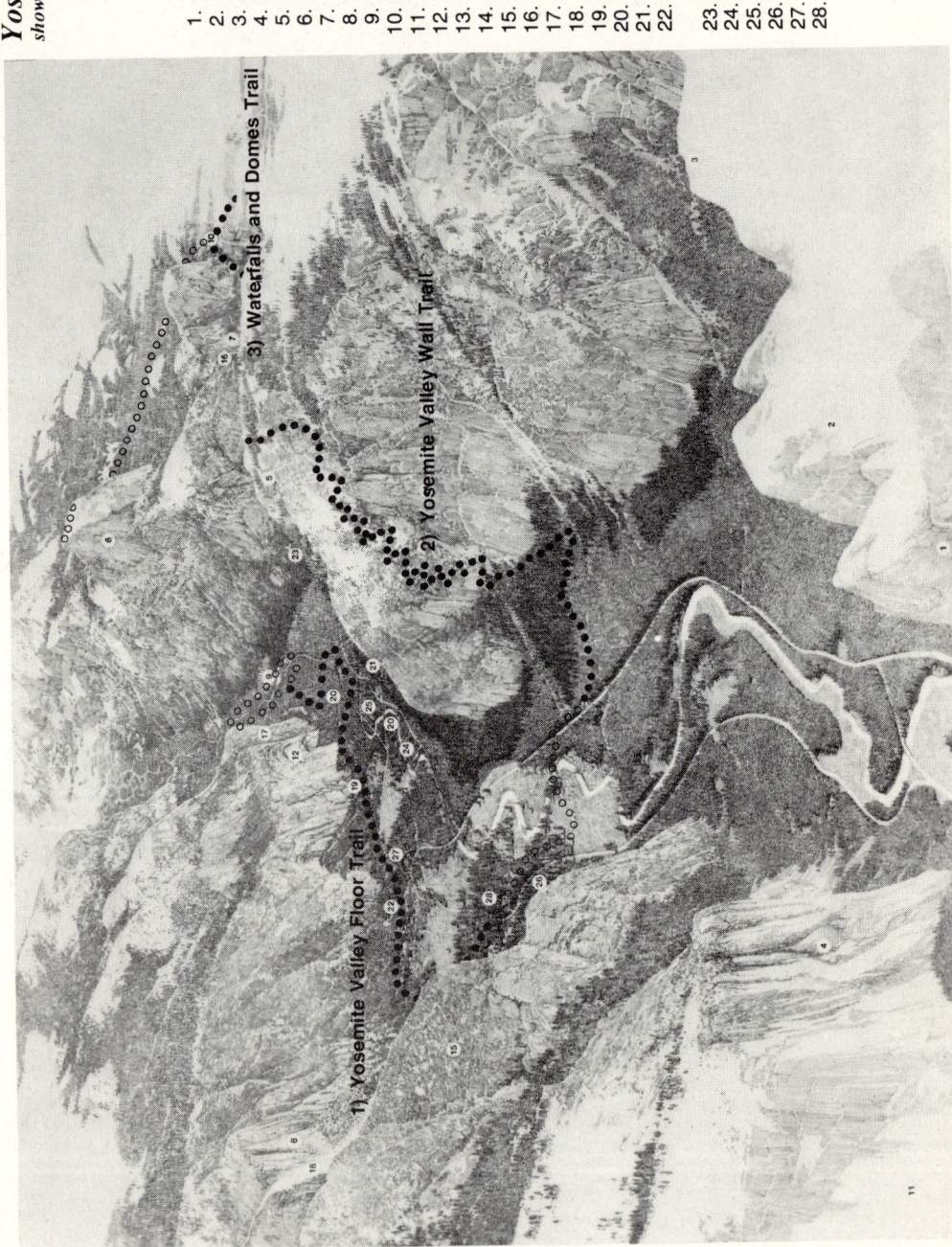

1) Yosemite Valley Floor Trail
2) Yosemite Valley Wall Trail
3) Waterfalls and Domes Trail

8

1) *YOSEMITE VALLEY FLOOR*
Lower Yosemite Fall to Mirror Lake

Start: Lower Yosemite Fall parking area (3,960 feet)

Finish: Mirror Lake shuttlebus stop (4,100 feet)

Elevation gain: 140 feet

Distance: 4.1 miles

Time: 3 hours

Seasons: all

Map: Centerfold, pages 38-40

Yosemite Falls

A walk through Yosemite Valley provides constantly varying perspectives of scenery unique on Earth, passing more waterfalls and taller cliffs than exist in any other location. You can look up the 3,000-foot face of El Capitan, see Bridalveil Fall drop as though direct from the sky, and in spring get drenched by the spray from roaring Lower Yosemite Fall. Between these world supremes you'll find more attractions — Indian caves and mortar rocks, river rapids and placid pools, ponderosa pine forests and chickaree tree squirrels.

Why is Yosemite Valley so unusual? It is so appealing that as early as 1864, only 13 years after its discovery, President Ab-

North Dome and Half Dome above the Merced River, winter

raham Lincoln signed the law setting it aside as a scenic and natural preserve, the first such in the world. At that time its origin was unknown, but soon a theory was developed by Professor Josiah Whitney that the valley had formed when its bottom fell out and Half Dome split in two, the lost half having dropped into the abyss, filling that to its present level. Later, however, John Muir showed that thick glaciers had formed in the High Sierra and descended pre-existing stream valleys to enter the Yosemite and carve it out. When the last of these glaciers melted, a basin was left scooped in the valley floor. This then filled with water to become Ancient Lake Yosemite, as time passed reflecting the retreat of the ice cascades and the birth of the waterfalls, until it filled in with sediment and vanished, leaving only a flat sandy floor filling with grasses and forest trees.

Indians came to live on this fruitful land, gathering acorns from the oaks, seeds from the meadow grasses, basketry materials from the ferns, and deer from the forests, changing the land or their ways little for thousands of years more. Finally, however, '49er miners, rushing into the Mother Lode gold country just west, came into conflict with the original inhabitants. The result was the Mariposa Indian War, the

the original inhabitants, depicted by an early artist

discovery of Yosemite Valley, and the removal of most of the Indians — by 1851. Shortly, tourist travel began and then increased, inspired by and also inspiring in turn the awakening pre-1900 enthusiasm for natural landscapes.

Yosemite Valley is thus a flat-floored gorge about seven miles long east-west, and less than a mile wide. Within, an elongate loop trail follows the base of the valley walls on both sides, and a road loop fits concentrically inside that. Down through the center of all flows the Merced River, with bridges over it connecting north and south. Short spur trails lead from the road loop outward to important features, and most visitors use only these spurs, riding

glacier in Yosemite Valley

Ancient Lake Yosemite, 30,000 years ago

Lower Yosemite Fall above Yosemite Creek and bridge

between them by car or bus. But you can take the trail loop instead and both see the world-famous sights and also enjoy the quiet interludes of trail between them. Because of the bus system in the valley and the alternate trails that are available, you seldom need to retrace your steps. You can nagivate like an Indian, keeping track of your location by the landmarks towering high all about. But the map in the center of this book will also help.

Perhaps the finest stretch of this valley loop trail is between Yosemite Falls and Mirror Lake. From the parking area on the road loop opposite Yosemite Lodge and west of the arched stone Yosemite Creek bridge, you can head for the fall on foot, in plain view, the base ¼ mile away. Closer, the cliff blocks out the Upper Fall and only the Lower is seen. The Lower alone is 320 feet tall; combined with the Upper (1,430 feet) and including some cascades between, the total drop from the upland rim is 2,425 feet, making this the second highest waterfall in the world (Angel Falls in Venezuela is higher). Watch the individual comet-shaped masses of water fan partly into spray in their descent, big drops whipped by the wind as they fall through space.

Where the trail approaches the Lower Fall most closely, cross over Yosemite Creek, walking east toward the head of the valley. The waters flowing under the bridge here are the same you have just watched in the sky. In winter and spring, frazil ice is sometimes present. Then the waterfall spray, chilled below freezing from its drop through the cold air, collects in the Creek's water, causing it to congeal, the whole first becoming a sluggishly flowing slurry which then turns on the surface to porous white ice particles but often remains still partly fluid inside. This frazil ice may be many feet deep, hiding the bridge, if it has not removed it, and is hazardous to walk on, especially when fresh. It seems quite out of place at times when there is no snow in the valley and prompts visitors unfamiliar with the phenomenon to ask why snow would fall only at the base of the falls.

Autumn is quite another season for Yosemite Falls. The waterfall often runs dry by then, a trait which initially caused Horace Greeley to brand it a "humbug" on his 1859 trip west, although he later changed his opinion.

Continuing eastward on the foot trail, in 0.2 mile the horsetrail branching to the right leads back in 0.4 mile to the Lower Fall parking area, passing close to the unmarked site where John Muir built a sawmill along a distributary of Yosemite Creek, living in an attic room there for a

frazil ice, Yosemite Creek below Falls

John Muir's Yosemite Creek cabin (as shown on placque)

time. A memorial plaque and bench is not far, with this quotation from Muir, which could well serve as the theme for this book:

"Climb the mountains and get their
   good tidings.
Nature's peace will flow into you
   as sunshine flows into trees.
The winds will blow their own freshness
   into you,
and the storms their energy,
while cares will drop off like autumn
   leaves."

Mirror Lake, by our route, is 3.6 miles from this junction. Our trail now passes behind the government housing provided for National Park Service employees, and in 0.2 mile comes to the NPS maintenance area. Behind the horse corral here an opening in the forest reveals a talus slope (rock rubble) leading up the valley wall to Sunnyside Bench. Experienced rock climbers can go up this slope and follow the bench, marked by brush and trees, horizontally back to the top of Lower Yosemite Fall. They also can take a more difficult route upward to Fern Ledge on the Upper Yosemite Fall cliff, a favorite haunt of John Muir, and one where he was once bombarded by the water column when wind swayed it over him, nearly washing him away. Note here the Lost Arrow column standing free from the cliff above you, left of Yosemite Point. Also note across the valley on the opposite (south) wall, Glacier Point (left) and Sentinel Rock (right).

The trail, climbing upward onto the talus slope under live oak trees and then dropping, in 0.4 mile crosses on the bridge over Indian Creek, which runs only in spring — at that season draining the steep Indian Canyon above. The Ahwahneechee Indian people used cliffs on the right side of this canyon to pass in and out of the valley in the days when their Mono Trail was the principal route across the Sierra Nevada in this region. Over it, acorns moved eastward, and arrowhead-quality obsidian and salt from the desert came west. Their word *uzumati,* meaning grizzly bear, was adapted by the white man's tongue to Yosemite.

Beyond Indian Creek 0.2 mile is Church Bowl and Ahwahnee Meadow. Views from here across the opening to Glacier Point and Monday Morning Slab (the sloping apron of rock below it) are good. The upper cliffs of Glacier Point are of a kind of granitic rock (called Sentinel granodiorite) different from that composing the lower slab (Half Dome quartz monzonite). In this part of the valley, the glacier dug 2,000 feet below the present meadow surface. As Glacier Point stands over 3,000 feet above the meadow level, and the ice extended

Lost Arrow spire

above that, ice fully a mile thick once flowed past this spot.

The rock type has changed on our trail's side of the valley, too, and now the cliffs are formed of the same kind of massive granite as is Monday Morning Slab. Consequently, arch formations show here on the Valley walls (Little Royal Arches and Royal Arches) and massive North Dome stands out of sight above them atop the wall.

We go on 0.3 mile beyond Church Bowl, passing The Ahwahnee hotel between the talus (rock rubble) below the granite wall and the hotel access road.

About 70 yards beyond the eastern edge of the hotel parking area, a series of poorly-defined use routes scramble steeply up to the left 100 yards over talus and then 100 yards up to the right along ledges out to the Devils Bathtub. Add half an hour to your trip time if you decide to go out to here, a series of water pockets at the refreshing end of the Royal Arch Cascade which slides down the wall from above. (Avoid this area when runoff is high; it will be dangerous.) Views up and down the valley are good from here, as the perch is well above the treetops. Several delicate flowers and ferns grow near the moisture supply. The water should be good to drink where running, as upstream is only pure wilderness. Because of the stream action on it, the rock here is polished, and slick even when dry. Thus you can see its internal characteristics well. This is the Half Dome quartz monzonite, showing its typical dark hornblende crystals and black "books" of biotite mica in six-sided stacks of loose flakes within the groundmass of pale white and gray feldspars mixed with clear quartz.

Back on the main trail, in 0.1 mile beyond The Ahwahnee hotel, Half Dome appears ahead through the forest, and in another 0.1 mile is a good view up to the Royal Arches.

Next, a trail forks off on the right (south) heading for the Stables. We take this in order to see Medial Moraine in the valley center. (At times when the shuttlebus does not operate to Mirror Lake, it will be more efficient to go directly to Indian Caves — 0.5 mile beyond this trail fork — then to Mirror Lake, returning on the trail on the south side of Tenaya Creek to Medial Moraine and the shuttlebus stop at the Stables.) Turn south and cross the paved bicycle path immediately adjacent to the junction, and in 0.1 mile cross on the bridge over Tenaya Creek. Follow the trail along this stream, passing North Pines Campground. Pass on the right (west) of the stables, heading on the trail for the Merced River, but just before reaching the bridge (Clarks), turn left (east) toward Half Dome, and begin ascending the low forested hill before you, leaving the trail. Ridge-shaped, this is Medial Moraine. Composed of loose debris dropped by the last glacier to enter Yosemite Valley, it contains both sand and boulders, including a number of rocks of types entirely foreign to its site. Of these "erratics", the most dramatic is a rock with prominent knobs projecting from its surface; these are large crystals of the mineral feldspar, and the

Medial Moraine – with Cathedral Peak granite boulders in foreground and Upper Yosemite Fall in background

13

rock is the Cathedral Peak granite — named for its origin in the mountains over 8 miles away, near Tuolumne Meadows. Walk along the top or left (north) slope of this ridge, with excellent views of North Dome to the left and peeks through the trees back (west) at Yosemite Falls. At the eastern end, cross the road and turn left (north) on the trail just beyond it. [If this is hard for you to find, just turn left (north) onto the shuttlebus road, then right (east) at the first fork.] Both trail and road soon cross Tenaya Creek at the road bridge, just before which (south of) there is a junction with another trail to the left (west) heading back to the stables and a trail to the right (east) heading up the south bank of Tenaya Creek to Mirror Lake. After crossing the bridge, we leave the road on a trail headed north toward Washington Column (looming above Indian Caves), there rejoining the trail along the north valley wall.

Indian Caves are formed in the void spaces below immense blocks of rock that have fallen — and still fall — from the cliffs above. An Indian camp with one lone old woman was observed here in 1851 when the valley was first entered by Mother Lode miners organized as the Mariposa

Indian women pounding acorns

Battalion. They were determined to stop the Yosemite tribe from troubling them, but failing to capture them, resorted to burning the Indians' food supplies and dwellings. The Indians lived in the caves here and in bark and pole shelters, storing the acorns from the black oaks in specially built caches. On the sloping top of the large rock nearby, the squaws ground these acorns into flour for mush or "cookies". Explore in and around the caves if you like, but use caution because some of them require flashlights and regular cave exploring techniques. The next large rock upslope from the bedrock mortar is split in two. Walk along either side of it — or through it — to see the open crack.

A shuttlebus stop — in season — is on the road nearby to the right (south) if you wish to abort your trip here.

Now climb gently 140 feet up the trail to Mirror Lake (0.7 mile). In spring, Mirror Lake reflects Mount Watkins on the left side of the canyon and the unique Half Dome on the right. Because canyon winds change twice a day — from upcanyon to downcanyon at dusk, and vice versa at dawn — winds are at those times most likely to be still and the reflecting surface unruffled. Ice coats the lake in winter, but only rarely is it thick enough for walking on or skating over. By late summer the delta

North Dome above Royal Arches and Washington Column

Tenaya Canyon above Mirror Lake – Mount Watkins on left, Half Dome's lower slope on right.

entering with Tenaya Creek is above water (if any water is present at all), showing how the lake has been nearly filled in to a "Mirror Meadow" since the first photos a century ago. The forested flat upstream from the lake was similarly filled long before that. Thus Mirror Lake is in this regard like the ancient lake formerly in Yosemite Valley. Yet Mirror Lake is not glacial. The Ice Age ended here so long ago that Tenaya Creek would have filled the small lake in with sand by now. Instead, the lake formed when a huge rockfall dropped into Tenaya Canyon from the Half Dome or North Dome slopes above, damming the stream.

At the upper end of the lake is a fine vantage for looking at Tenaya Canyon, showing well the U-shaped gorge typical of glaciated mountain valleys. Continue along the use trail around the left (north) lakeshore and then follow the constructed trail where the lake, widening, forces the two trails to join. At 0.1 mile beyond, where the trail comes closest to the valley wall, a side path (which may be obscure and unmarked) leads to the left and up the slope a few hundred feet to fine glacial polish and horizontal striae (scratches) on the granite.

This completes the Yosemite Falls to Mirror Lake hike. Walk on the constructed trail back to the Mirror Lake shuttlebus stop where in season you may catch a ride to other points in the valley.

Or, if you want to go on up Tenaya Canyon now (or return later to do so), take the 3-mile loop trail that continues beyond Mirror Lake up the canyon on the left (northwest) side, crosses Tenaya Creek, and returns on the other (southeast) side. Allow 2 hours additional for this jaunt. In winter this loop can be hazardous during and after major snowstorms, because avalanches from the steep slopes above are frequent — as often as one per minute at times, and do occasionally reach the trail.

Horsetail rush is common at places where the trail swings low alongside Tenaya Creek. Some of the trees are Douglas-fir (on the talus), white fir, incense-cedar, dogwood, and black oak.

At 1.1 miles past Mirror Lake, the trail to May Lake and Tenaya Lake leaves on the left (north) side. A climb of ¼ mile up this takes you through and then above the live oak forest there to open views of Clouds Rest, Half Dome, and Quarter Dome on the south side of Tenaya Canyon; of Basket Dome above on this side; and of Tenaya Fall in the canyon bottom.

Back at the loop trail, Tenaya Creek now descends by rapids and pools and in season is boisterous and noisy. It is 0.3 mile on to where the spur to Snow Creek leaves to the left.

This Snow Creek spur extends out 0.2 mile, turning left up this side of the creek shortly before ending. From there, cautious scramblers can continue up open rock slopes on the left (west) bank to a spot where, during the runoff season, a lower drop of Snow Creek Falls shoots out in a fantastic arc. (This is seen before the steep cliffs and without doing any rock climbing per se.)

Again back at the loop trail, proceed onward 100 yards to the bridge over Tenaya Creek.

Just at the far (south) end of this Tenaya

Creek bridge, a difficult use trail exits to the left leading upstream 0.2 mile to Tenaya Falls, low falls for Yosemite and rather concealed by large trees and boulders. Ferns and some large black oaks grow below this waterfall, and it is a likely spot for water ouzels and their moss nests. During spring high water use great care on this side trip near the stream and on slippery rocks; later in the season you may be able to cross the river and return on the opposite bank to the trail (or go up that shore).

Now begin the return on the trail down the southeast side of the canyon. Views of Basket Dome are best from this side, and you should saunter out to sit on a log in one of the meadow openings. Deer might be seen. Explore the head of Mirror Lake and the sand and gravel delta, but you normally won't be able to cross the inlet creek here as it runs still and deep entering the lake. You can cross back to the road side of the lake at the outlet during low water, or continue downstream beyond to the lower end of the pond in sight (dry in late summer). From there turn right off the main horse trail, cross the footbridge over Tenaya Creek and walk up the road 0.2 mile back to the Mirror Lake shuttlebus stop (in season), or down the road 0.5 mile to the Indian Caves shuttlebus stop. At the shuttlebus stops catch a ride to other points in the valley. Or, you may continue on the horse trail on the south side of Tenaya Creek to Medial Moraine and the shuttle bus stop at the Stables.

South Yosemite Valley wall with Sentinel Rock and approximate route of descent of 4-Mile Trail

2) THE VALLEY WALL
Glacier Point to Yosemite Valley Floor

Start: Glacier Point parking area (7,200 feet)

Finish: Yosemite Valley 4-Mile Trail parking area (3,980 feet) on south valley road, 1.8 miles east of El Capitan crossroad

Elevation gain: 200 feet

Elevation loss: 3,420 feet

Distance: 4.7 miles one-way downhill.

Time: 3 hours

Water: None

Seasons: Summer, fall

Map: Centerfold, pages 38-40

Glacier Point cliff with Overhanging Rock – Half Dome beyond

Glacier Point is the platform for viewing Yosemite — with the Valley below, Half Dome and the Giant's Stairway of Vernal and Nevada Falls opposite, and the High Sierra rising to the range crest beyond. It is a viewpoint outstanding in the world for glacial, granitic scenery, and is perched atop one of the world's highest and sheerest dropoffs.

All these things are seen from the very top of this trail. Following it down the south valley wall, however, provides new angles for viewing the scene and so opens new perspectives. The hike also shows how life zones or plant communities change in such a descent — from the red fir coniferous forest of 7,000 feet elevation to the valley floor mixed conifer and deciduous forest at 4,000 feet. Temperatures rise on the way down, too, most days.

This south wall, shaded by the plateau behind, gets less sun to warm and dry it than does the wall on the north side of Yosemite Valley. Consequently, winter snows linger here longer.

The trail is historic, built in 1870-71, immediately becoming a major route into Yosemite Valley as there were no access roads even for stagecoaches then. Called the 4-Mile Trail, it is actually 4.7 miles long, lengthened by trail improvements over the years since the initial construction and naming. Soon after it was completed, other trails and a stagecoach road were built to Glacier Point, but in spite of this varied access, it was planned as early as 1887 to provide as well a mechanical passenger lift from the valley, a proposal since repeated many times and always controversial. A Mountain House was built at this early time, and later the Glacier Point Hotel. Both burned in 1969, ending the period when overnight accommodations could be had here.

Hike this trail downhill! Get a ride to Glacier Point, take a bus, or arrange a car shuttle, and try Yosemite hiking in reverse! You'll find you wind less, but may tire as easily, so don't forget to stop and rest occasionally. Have good knees for the many, many down-steps.

You begin on the path to the main Glacier Point viewing area from the parking lot, bearing left at the trail fork just past

Glacier Point view: Tenaya Canyon, Half Dome, Vernal and Nevada Falls

the concession stand. But first go 0.1 mile north to the cliff edge (not 0.2 mile!) and see the world-famous view straight down the 3,200-foot precipice to Yosemite Valley below, maplike from this height. A four-acre historic apple orchard, the trees twenty feet apart, appears as a checkerboard. Left of this point is Overhanging Rock (fenced off now) where early tourists posed for photographs above the abyss, some even standing there on their heads or kicking high in long dresses. On the side of the promontory toward Half Dome is a geological observatory and a peak identifier, as well as the best views of that dome, of Tenaya Canyon, and of Vernal and Nevada Falls in the Giant's Stairway.

Imagine a glacier filling the entire valley clear up to where you are standing, and higher still — because one did. It scoured the floor of the Valley out deeper than you can see and trimmed the cliff walls back, and when the Ice Age ended it left a lake shimmering the length and breadth of Yosemite Valley. A branch of this ice stream descended where Nevada and Vernal Falls are now and another was in Tenaya Canyon to the left of Half Dome. Only Half Dome's top and the Cloud's Rest ridge behind stood above these glaciers, dividing them.

An early-day visitor enjoying the view from Overhanging Rock (not encouraged)

Return to the 4-Mile Trail and start descending gradually through the forest, passing a variety of conifers (red and white firs, sugar and Jeffrey pines), crossing the Staircase Creek drainage. In spring this stream drops in successive leaps down stepped ledges in the valley wall as Staircase Falls behind Curry Village. The historic Ledge Trail, a steep 1.75 miles, came up an exposed route from the valley floor to here. After many years of use marred by frequent tragic accidents, this route was finally removed from the park's trail system and travel on it is now in the category of mountaineering.

Some of the best views of Half Dome and Tenaya Canyon are had near this upper stretch of the 4-Mile Trail. Also from these upper areas, someone once thought North Dome across the valley looked like a sculpted profile of George Washington's head. Somehow this resulted in the name for Washington Column, the pillar just below George's "chin", perhaps because this granite rock shaft resembles the pedestal such a gigantic bust would need to sit on, or

George Washington in profile?

perhaps because it resembles the Washington Monument spire in our national capitol.

After a slight climb, at a point about 0.7 mile from Glacier Point the trail begins its long continuous descent to the valley floor. At many places where the trail switches back there are excellent views across the valley. These vistas show well the two horizontal fracture lines in the granite wall behind Yosemite Falls, marked by the brush and trees that grow along them. The lower line, Sunnyside Bench, is at the top of the Lower Yosemite Fall and forms a mountaineering route to the fall's brink. The upper line is at the base of the Upper Yosemite Fall, and just left of that fall this line widens out to a cave visible at low-flow times. (Note that this upper line, especially — which is the trace on the granite surface of the fracture plane within — is not straight but is indented in a broad curve by the water fall recess. This is because you are looking down on the horizontal fracture plane; lower on this trail where you are even with the plane and cannot see the fall's recess so clearly, the line will seem straight.) Together, these two master fractures of the Yosemite granites have determined the particular configuration of the two Yosemite Falls. Note also the patches of gray color that arc to the left of the base of the Upper Fall. Vertical slabs of granite (exfoliation plates parallel to the steep cliff) have scaled off the wall in the past few years.

Descend a brushy chinquapin- and manzanita-covered slope over switchbacks for a mile to Union Point. The fire marks — healing now — in the forest above the trail and east of Sentinel Rock date from dry 1968, when an early summer fire raged up the slope from an out-of-bounds campfire. Up and east from Union Point a trail once led to Moran Point, a well-known vista of early days named for Thomas Moran, famous landscape painter of the late 1800s who did a painting of Half Dome and Yosemite Valley from there. His works on Yosemite, Yellowstone, Grand Canyon, Grand Teton, and other western landscapes helped inspire the national park idea, and he has been called "the father of our national parks." Union Point is reached 1.9 miles from the trail top, 2.8 miles still to go to the bottom. (If your intent is to return to the trail top rather than go clear to the bottom, this is a good turnaround spot, after enjoying the view and resting, as the trail continues steeply from here and the best views have already been had. Be sure to read the rest of this trail's description before starting back, however.)

Just east of Union Point, below the trail, 85-foot high Agassiz Column stands pre-

Yosemite Falls cliff showing horizontal fracture lines at base of Upper Fall and at top of Lower Fall. Zigzags of trail to top show in brushy gully left of Upper Fall.

Agassiz Column at Union Point

cariously balanced on a crumbling base, its prismatic form determined wholly by intersecting joint planes, vertical and oblique, the last remnant of a larger rock mass that was divided by many such fractures. The column is named for Louis Agassiz, "father of glacial geology". Although Agassiz never visited Yosemite, such a reminder of this man is appropriate here: It was regarding this valley that one of his "disciples" (John Muir) so effectively did battle with and overturned the then-established theory of the valley's formation — that its bottom had dropped out and Half Dome had split in two, the lost half having fallen in.

Looking down into Yosemite Valley toward the west, you'll see the Merced River cutting through Leidig Meadow, and north of the riverbank is an old meander oxbow marking a former channel. Now the river is stabilized by rockwork, and these natural floodmarks are filling in.

If you began your trip later in the day, the descent from here will be in the declining sun, with the whole western end of the valley being brought into brilliant relief. After about a mile more of switchbacking below Union Point, the trail heads left on a southwest line down a steady grade, crossing a creek on the talus slope and then passing under the great face of Sentinel Rock. Maples may be noticed in this vicinity. Here major snow avalanches slide across the trail in winter, booming down from the steep and vertical cliffs above, pruning the trees. This is a hazard not only during that season but also creates another harzard until late some springs (even June) because the immense snow piles left may not melt away before then, keeping the trail impassable or unsafe to hikers without technical ice climbing equipment and skills.

At the end of this straight stretch, a mile long itself, it is another mile, now through live oak woods, to the bottom of the trail. At the bottom is the Yosemite Valley mixed conifer forest — with ponderosa pine, white fir, and black oak — a totally different plant community from that at the top, the 3,200-foot descent representing the same climatic change as a 500 mile journey south. How are your knees and the ends of your toes? They may feel like they have gone the full 500 miles!

Also at the trail bottom is the site of the first tourist accommodations that were built in Yosemite Valley, beginning in 1865 and lasting until 1888 when the Yosemite commissioners directed that this area be cleared. The Yosemite Chapel, now up the valley near Sentinel Bridge, was originally built here (in 1879). Moved to get it into the new Upper Village, that village eventually became the Old Village, and now it has virtually been eliminated, too, in the continuing effort to locate needed facilities where they least interfere with the valley views and are less subject to flood damage and the cold shade of winter under cliffs. At this Lower Village, where we are now,

Merced River in Yosemite Valley, with abandoned "oxbow" channel near center

View west down Yosemite Valley from 4-Mile Trail past Sentinel Rock (on left) to Cathedral Rocks (in center) and El Capitan (on right)

there was also Black's Lower Hotel, Leidig's Hotel (Leidig Meadow is across the river from here, where the cows grazed), Camp Ahwahnee, laundry, meat market, stables, and photographic studio. See if you can find the locust trees at the site of an old well, all that now remains of this village.

John Muir was living here at Black's when he experienced the great Yosemite earthquake of March 26, 1872. Running out of his cabin under Sentinel Rock, he shouted "A noble earthquake! A noble earthquake!", fearing that Sentinel Rock itself was going to be shattered, but feeling sure he "was going to learn something." It was 2:30 a.m., with moonlight. Soon Eagle Rock, half a mile up the valley on this side, gave way, its thousands of great boulders "pouring to the Valley floor in a free curve luminous from friction . . . an arc of glowing, passionate fire, fifteen hundred feet span." To Muir, "The sound was so tremendously deep and broad and earnest, the whole earth like a living creature seemed to have at last found a voice and to be calling to her sister planets."

Huge fir trees were snapped off and a large area was covered with a rubble pile many feet thick, much of it bare of vegetation still. If you look back up the south wall on either side of Sentinel Falls, you will see raw spots on the cliff, indicating that the 1872 slide was not the last one. A rockfall from there in 1949 wiped out 600 feet of the trail you just descended, burying it 2 to 6 feet deep with loose rock debris and nearly reaching the valley floor. Mature trees were splintered or sheared off while others were left standing stark beneath the cliff shorne of all their branches. The grating rocks created so much dust that a gray particle-cloud rose to the valley rim, blotting out the sun, enveloping horseback riders and picnickers, and making breathing difficult.

From here, if you don't have a car parked, walk east upvalley on the south trail 0.3 mile to a junction and turn left (north) across the south valley road and then cross the Merced River on the foot and horse bridge, following the wide path (an old road) 0.7 mile back to Yosemite Lodge, bearing right there to the shuttlebus stop. Alternatively, to reach the shuttlebus stop north of Sentinel Bridge, after walking east upvalley on the south trail 0.3 mile to the junction with the trail to the Lodge, continue on the south trail 0.8 mile past the Chapel and through the Old Village to and across the Merced River, stopping at the large parking area just north.

Sentinel Rock, behind Black's Hotel, where John Muir observed earthquake of 1872. Sketched by Muir.

3) WATERFALLS AND DOMES
Vernal-Nevada Falls with Half Dome option

	Elevation gain, feet	Elevation loss, feet	Distance miles	Time hours
Start and finish: Happy Isles (4,035 feet)				
One-way Happy Isles to top of Nevada Fall (5,907 feet)	2,005	100	2.7	4
One-way return to Happy Isles	40	1,945	3.5	2
Round-trip totals:	2,045	2,045	6.2	6
One-way Happy Isles to top of Half Dome (8,842) feet)	4,845	100	7.0	8
One-way return to Happy Isles	40	4,785	8.2	4
Round-trip totals:	4,885	4,855	15.2	12

Map: Centerfold, pages 38-40

Winter—Ice may coat Mist Trail below Vernal Fall and coat or completely block horse trail west of Nevada Fall; snow may be deep; snow avalanches may cross trails.

Spring—Highest water flow, so carry raingear and protect lunches and cameras or get soaked on Mist Trail below Vernal Fall; snow avalanches may cross trails.

Water: Carry on longer hikes. Available at trail start, fountain at Vernal Falls Bridge, at spring near ridgetop below Half Dome. Heavy use of this area makes main river suspect of purity.

Notes for Half Dome climb: Be in top shape, start at dawn, or first backpack overnight (with wilderness permit) to Little Yosemite Valley. Half Dome is climbed in summer via a cable route, dismantled every autumn to avoid damage from snow avalanches and icefall and not reassembled until late each spring. Always check on its status. Expect

Giant's Stairway with Vernal Fall (lower) and Nevada Fall; Liberty Cap between at left.

technical rock climb if cables are not up. Stay off Half Dome during rain-, snow-, or lightning-storm.

In this little section of Yosemite is the finest waterfall and stream scenery anywhere, the whole capped by a unique half of a dome. You may have already seen into this terrain from Glacier Point; now you

Yosemite Falls from Vernal Fall Trail; Glacier Point apron on left.

have a chance to explore it intimately. It is aptly called the Giant's Stairway, for from a mammoth perspective the ascent has fairly even treads with two distinct risers — Vernal and Nevada Falls. At such a scale, it is thus only two steps to the top of Nevada Fall, and a third one (big even for a giant) to the top of Half Dome.

The entire canyon here was filled with ice during the glacial period, the cold streams so deep they even buried the lower ¾ of Half Dome. In the canyon, they left their polish on the bedrock, dropped erratic boulders of Cathedral Peak granite brought down from the Tuolumne Meadows area, and quarried away the bedrock where they could. They widened out the canyon noticeably, for the streambed today occupies only a small portion of the wide glacial gorge. The Vernal and Nevada Falls cliffs were left where they are now because their rock was tougher, bearing fewer fractures than did the rock now holding the treads. In this case, strength begot strength, for once the stairway risers began to develop under the glacier, the tendency was for them to remain and even be heightened as the ice descended with greater force onto the receding treads below. Thus the analogy with the giant remains appropriate, for a giant person, like the giant ice stream, would also wear the treads and not the risers. And so shall we wear only the treads of the smaller trail steps as we ascend at our scale.

Arrive at Happy Isles trailhead by walking or via the shuttlebus. Restrooms, drinking water, Nature Center, and snacks are available here in season. North Dome is seen down the Merced River from the concrete bridge, on the north wall of Yosemite Valley, and watch here for a dipper (or water-ouzel) — a slate-grey terrestrial bird fond of streams — in the current itself or bobbing on a nearby rock.

Cross the concrete bridge over the Merced River and start up the John Muir Trail, steep soon and for most of the way to the top of Nevada Fall. In 0.1 mile the alternate trail from Happy Isles to this trail joins from below on the right.

Near this point, an unmarked and now-abandoned route goes to Sierra Point. This overlook was named for the Sierra Club, and was selected to give a view of five major Yosemite waterfalls from one place:

Illilouette Fall in its canyon

fracture lines at Yosemite Falls marked by the brush and trees that grow along them. The sloping apron below Glacier Point (on the left) is Monday Morning Slab, also seen from other vantages. This slab is made of granite different from that in the steeper cliffs high above it (Sentinel granodiorite) but the same as the granitic rock here at our viewpoint (Half Dome quartz monzonite) and continuously up the trail clear to the top of Half Dome and beyond.

The trail climbs more, passing in 0.1 mile a view to the right of Illilouette Fall (370 feet high), recessed in its gorge. Then we descend on the trail to the bridge across the Merced River, 0.8 mile from our start. Toilets and drinking water are here. Now the river is choked with huge talus boulders fallen from the cliffs above. These give an excellent foreground for viewing Vernal Fall, seen over a half mile of foaming cascades.

Beyond the bridge 0.2 mile the horse trail (built by Albert Snow in 1870) begins a

Vernal, Nevada, Illilouette, and Upper and Lower Yosemite Falls. Views from Sierra Point are best at the height of the waterfall season, of course. If taken, the trip should be a separate one — not a side trip on the way up the Giant's Stairway.

The route – a mountaineering route rather than a trail – exits obscurely to the left (uphill) 50 feet before (downhill from) a spring that once served a horse-watering trough on the main trail. It climbs very steeply 750 vertical feet eastward up the slope of Grizzly Peak to Sierra Point, in 0.5 mile. Expect to use your hands in several places in making this scramble – especially on the the return as downhill views always seem steeper – and don't get off the route as there are steep cliffs to its sides. The railing that has marked the end of the route at Sierra Point for many years may deteriorate now that the trail is abandoned. Retreat anywhere you are in doubt.

Ascending the main trail at 0.4 mile from Happy Isles, you see and hear the Merced River tumbling below, and, rounding a stone-masonry walled corner there is a good view back into Yosemite Valley. From here you see again the two horizontal

Anderson ascending Half Dome, 1875

tollkeeper's cabin at Register Rock, 1800s

circuitous uphill route to the right, on which we will later return. Going up, however, our trail is the Mist Trail, with Vernal Fall 0.3 mile straight ahead. At this spot a tollkeeper once extracted a dollar fare for passage beyond, holding forth under nearby large Register Rock.

Up the trail 0.1 mile, on its left side, the large Lady Franklin Rock (with one side in the river current) provides an excellent view of the Fall, one in use over a century.

Soon you'll see why horses aren't used on the Mist Trail. A rock stairway begins, with over 500 steps to the top, plus many fine places to pause, view, and rest. From here mist from Vernal Fall will soak or refresh you depending on the season and

Vernal Fall

your frame of mind. Protect cameras, papers, and lunches and be rested for the upstairs dash that is often necessary past the wettest stretch. A large rock provides partial shelter from the rain partway up. Look for brilliant rainbows in the mist, even double or circular ones. The green slope of tender, moisture-loving plants in the spray zone below the trail gave Vernal Fall its name.

Once, George Anderson, who in 1875 was the first to climb Half Dome and in 1882 built the trail you used from Happy Isles to Vernal Fall Bridge, tried to get a stagecoach road up the canyon slope on the opposite side of the river from our trail. He built most of it, much of it still there in the live-oak woods, but the Fall cliff stopped his effort. Why he didn't anticipate this obstacle is curious today, perhaps an illustration of the pioneer spirit — optimistic in spite of odds truly insurmountable.

At the top of Vernal Fall the dashing water has a clean, foam-flecked, mottled light to dark apple-green color before it hurtles outward over the level brink and then drops in a thundering white sheet. Do remember here and at Nevada Fall above

up Vernal Fall in 1872

La Casa Nevada, 1870-1890; Nevada Fall beyond

that moving water has great force, that granite is slick, that wet granite is slicker, and that the wet granite under the water here is stream-polished and slicker still. Don't join the hapless people and at least one bear who have suffered the extreme of short-lived embarrassment when they slipped and went over these falls, in some cases resulting in multiple tragedies when friends tried to help. If you brought children with you, watch them closely here.

Upriver 0.1 mile is Emerald Pool — large, but not so large that the river can't occasionally clean it out during floods. It occupies a depression formed in the granite by the scooping of an Ice Age glacier. At its head the Merced River washes as a sheet over a sloping rock slab wider than the riverbed, known as the Silver Apron. High-risk swimmers sometimes slide down the smoother lower part, but not all are able to avoid the rocks when they splash into the pool at the bottom; many have been injured. Often currents shoot up from this slab where they hit a slight obstruction and are deflected upward, rolling over in "waterwheels."

Climbing, our trail is joined in 0.1 mile by a spur coming from the horse trail (which is on the slope above, 0.4 mile up this spur), and then it crosses the Diamond Cascades of the Merced River on a bridge above the Silver Apron. Another 0.2 mile on the next flat once stood La Casa Nevada, a trailside hotel opened in 1870. At the edge of this site near the river is the best front view of Nevada Fall, just off the trail atop a small cliff. A few bits of crockery remain in the soil as the only evidence at the site of the park's early tourist industry here.

Next our trail heads for switchbacks leading up the gorge at the left (north) side of Nevada Fall, and right at the bottom of this is the best side view of Nevada Fall. Here water comets are seen leaping from the waterfall lip and flying until they strike a sloping granite slab partway down, there breaking into streaming water, giving the column the appearance of being bent. Perhaps that is why the Indians called this fall *Yo-wy-we,* "Twisting Fall," although some records give credit for the name to the twist at the fall's top just before the leap. When you get up there you can judge history's story for yourself.

The little gorge the trail now climbs once carried part of the flow of the Merced River, then called the Liberty Cap Cascades, but a dam built by the La Casa Nevada proprietor in the 1870-80 era turned the current back into the fall. The park commissioners paid him $500 for thus "fixing the falls", although early writers then scorned this "job of tinkering one of God's masterpieces . . . the Yosemite waterworks . . . about the last branch of industry that even Yankee ingenuity would

Nevada Fall; trail ascends slot to left.

Half Dome cableway – in summer

be likely to undertake.'' Immense Douglas-fir trees stand alongside the trail, good umbrellas should it rain, for their drooping ''bottle-brush'' tassels collectively form shingles and conduct the water outward at least for a while.

At the top is the junction with the trail to Little Yosemite (one mile ahead and stretching on for 2½ miles more) and to Half Dome (4.5 miles and 2,850 feet of climbing to the top). Here you have come 2.5 miles from Happy Isles and have risen 1,970 feet. If you are not going on to either Little Yosemite or Half Dome, skip the next several paragraphs in *italics*, which apply to the Half Dome climb only.

For Half Dome, walk ahead 1.0 mile and turn left uphill (north) on the John Muir Trail, also called Sunrise Trail here. You are now in Little Yosemite, a smaller yet individual version of its larger cousin downstream. In 1.5 miles more, turn left again at the trail junction. Half Dome's summit is 2.0 miles beyond. Here in the forest you cross the several lateral moraines of the long-vanished Merced Glacier, showing the height of the ice at a later, lower stage of the repeated advances. Earlier, ice extended clear up to the top of the ridge you are climbing. About a mile up this slope and near its top at the divide with Tenaya Canyon, where you might least expect it, is a spring. This is the last water before the top of Half Dome, except early in the season when there might still be melting snow. A spur use trail leads 0.1 mile to the right (east) off the main trail to the spring. Go there and drink and fill your canteen – or expect to be uncomfortably thirsty and possibly even fatigued before your return here, as the climb beyond becomes steeper and increasingly exposed to the high-altitude sun and wind. Just beyond the junction with this water spur trail, the main trail swings left to follow along the ridge leading southwest to Half Dome, mostly up and with some stretches so steep as to prompt you to use your hands. There is a cable to hold to in places. Finally you reach a low dome and drop slightly to a saddle before the last bare-rock pitch to the summit, here seeing the cable route clearly for the first time. The open granite looks practically vertical from here, and it is 45° in places, too steep to stand on unaided.

Leading directly upward to the summit is a cable trailway 900 feet long and rising 400 feet vertically. It consists of two steel ropes about three feet apart suspended at arm height from pipes set in the rock. You ascend by walking between the ropes, holding on, and leaning out and away from the slope slightly so your shoe soles contact the smooth rock more squarely, improving their friction-holding power. Crossboards are set at the bases of pairs of pipes, at intervals of 10 to 20 feet, providing spots to pause, rest, and pass or be passed by other hikers. Do not, however, start this climb if the cables are down – as they are at least in fall, winter, and spring so they are not swept away by snow or ice avalanches sliding off the steep and bare granite. Without the cables, this is a technical rock climb. Also, do not start this climb if there is any chance of rain, which will make the granite too slick for safety; or of lightning, which has before and could again strike the dome summit and also follow the cables downward, stunning those in the path, or worse. Remember that you also have to come back down, so before you get up too far, turn around and try a few steps descending to see if that is comfortable enough for you; the exposure to the steep dropoff all around bothers some, and it is best to know whether it does you while still low enough to retreat in comfort. (You might find it easier to descend sideways over the steeper spots, holding with both hands to just one of the steel ropes.)

The top of Half Dome is a fairly level, large, open surface with but a few small trees. It is truncated by the great cliff which you can peer down from a rock overhanging space by 80 feet to Yosemite Valley, with Mirror Lake 4,748 feet below. In early summer, look up Tenaya Canyon to see Pywiack Cascade, gliding down some 600 feet vertically in the trough, and across to see Snow Creek Falls dropping down a slot in the wall between Basket Dome (left) and Mount Watkins (right). Anytime, see Mount Hoffman above on the north, Clouds Rest up the ridge to the east, Mount Starr King (a steep-sided dome) to the south, and Glacier Point and Sentinel Dome on the west, with El Capitan in Yosemite Valley beyond, and much, much more. When you have drunk your fill of this scenery, retrace your route and continue with the directions below.

To reach the top of Nevada Fall, turn at the junction atop the zigzags up from the Nevada Fall base, and walk 0.2 mile on nearly level terrain southwest to the top of Nevada Fall (toward Happy Isles and Yosemite Valley). On the way, you pass abundant glacial evidences — erratic boulders of rock different from the local Half Dome quartz monzonite, dropped there by the same moving ice that polished this bedrock smooth. To see Nevada Fall from the top, go down the steps to the railed viewing area on its right (northeast) side. Note the twisting channel *(Yo-wy-we?)*, the falling streamdrops, Emerald Pool, and Vernal Fall below (out of sight but often with a thin mist cloud at its top).

Cross the bridge over the Merced River above Nevada Fall and stay on this trail, the horse trail to Yosemite Valley, as you travel enjoying the views back of Nevada Fall, Liberty Cap on its left, Mount Broderick left of that, and the rounded back of Half Dome farther left still. Note that the gorges between these scenic formations run northwest-southeast parallel to the cliff face of Half Dome and therefore also parallel to the most common fracture system in the Sierra Nevada.

Beyond Nevada Fall 0.2 mile is the junction with the Panorama Trail to Glacier

1880 view of Liberty Cap and Nevada Fall, with La Casa Nevada on Knoll below

Point. Stay right. In 1.0 mile more near Clark's Point, on the right or downhill side, a connecting trail exits. This leads to a good view of Vernal Fall, to the Mist Trail (0.4 mile), and to the top of Vernal Fall (0.5 mile from here). You may take this route if you wish (it would cut 0.3 mile off your hike, but little or no time, as descending the Mist Trail stairway takes longer than the steady grade ahead on our trail). Continuing on the Horse Trail, it is 1.3 miles, descending by many switchbacks, to the junction with the Mist Trail at Register Rock, passed earlier today. From here it is 1.0 mile down the steep trail (rising for a stretch just after crossing the Merced River bridge) back to the start at Happy Isles.

When you get back to Happy Isles, avoid the temptation to rush back to civilization. Instead, 150 feet past the former horse-watering trough, take the less-used path that turns left downhill and leads via three wooden bridges across the Happy Isles islands themselves. It is no longer in distance than the main trail you followed earlier, and provides variety. Continue across the remaining bridges to the west bank of the Merced River and catch the shuttlebus at the loop-road stop nearby, or walk back on the Valley trail network to your camp or car.

But first find a rock beside the rushing water and sit and rest for a time to ponder the meaning then, in the time since, and today, of what Yosemite Guardian Walter Dennison wrote in 1885 when he named the Happy Isles: "No one can visit them without for the while forgetting the grinding strife of his world and being happy."

Happy Isles

4) GIANT SEQUOIAS / Mariposa Grove

Start: Tourbus stop at fallen Wawona Tunnel Tree, Upper Mariposa Grove (6,680 feet)

Finish: Parking area in Lower Grove (5,620 feet)

Elevation loss: 1,060 feet

Distance: 3.1 miles

Time: 2 hours

Seasons: All. Tourbus operates summer and fall; other times walk, ski, or snowshoe to start.

Map: page 37

Galen Clark at base of Grizzly Giant

Yosemite has three groves of giant sequoia trees, including some of the largest trees on Earth. Two of the groves — the Merced and the Tuolumne — are north of Yosemite Valley. The largest of the three is the Mariposa Grove, south of the valley near Wawona, yet even it is not nearly so large as those standing farther south in the Sierra in Sequoia National Park. (There is a sort of mini-grove in the park in the form of an isolated stand of the trees near Hetch Hetchy Valley, its history still not established.) A fourth local grove is outside the park not far from the Mariposa Grove, but it has been logged.

The giant sequoia has been of tremendous interest to humans since it became known. Once it was even thought to be the oldest living thing. But now the bristlecone pine has replaced it with that claim, yet the giant sequoia still retains the most popular interest. It is of course the largest living thing. It also has a fascinating life cycle, including its need as a seedling for fire in order to germinate, its ability to reproduce successfully from youth to old age, and, at maturity, its near-perfect defense from fire in the form of thick insulating bark (although the thin-barked young trees burn readily). Trees that live continue to produce viable seed for thirty and more centuries. The species thus accomplishes both the rapid succession of generations of young trees of but a few decades in age and also the nearly static presentation of unchanging genes from age-old specimens. The giant sequoia thus combines the best of the advantages gained from responding to changing conditions while retaining the proven advantages of its past successful life. One wonders what is the meaning of this species' survival mechanisms in a world of rapid environmental change. There may be lessons here for humans.

The giant sequoia's role in American and world conservation history is perhaps its greatest current significance. The environmental movement came late as it was, but it might not have come even then had the way not been paved. Ecological sensitivity all began with the desire to save this tree. The species was unknown before

1833, when the Walker party while crossing the Sierra noticed the trees of Yosemite's northern groves. The event went unheralded, however, because this group was looking for beaver to trap, not trees to cut. National prominence was afforded the species in the early 1850s when an immense tree in the Calaveras Grove farther north was stripped of its bark to be sent on exhibition, killing the tree for a purpose that was widely denounced in the nation's press, the first such outcry on a conservation issue.

Galen Clark explored the Mariposa Grove in 1857, coming up into it from his cabin at Wawona. By 1864 — during the Civil War — a bill was introduced into the U.S. Congress to set aside both Yosemite Valley and the Mariposa Grove. Although the valley is now the more famous, at that

Mariposa Grove in winter

giant sequoia cone and foliage

time the Congressmen in their testimony were concerned only about saving the big trees. President Lincoln signed the bill, the first of its kind in the world. Setting aside Yellowstone was the next significant conservation step, in 1872, but the very next time afterwards that Congress acted to save our natural heritage (in 1890), they set aside more sequoia groves at Sequoia National Park and enlarged Yosemite, including the Tuolumne and Merced Sequoia Groves. For once, the United States government was respectable in the eyes of its citizens. John Muir concluded in his *Our National Parks* in 1901,

> "Any fool can destroy trees. They cannot run away; and if they could, they would still be destroyed, — chased and hunted down as long as fun or a dollar could be got out of their bark hides, branching horns, or magnificent bole backbones. . . .

Through all the wonderful, eventful centuries before Christ's time — and long before that — God has cared for these trees, saved them from drought, disease, avalanches, and a thousand straining, leveling tempests and floods; but he cannot save them from fools, — only Uncle Sam can do that."

Today the National Park Service, over 300 areas strong and administrator of two percent of America — the best of its natural and cultural heritage, still sports a giant sequoia cone symbol in silver on its official uniform hatband. Look closely at the broad-brimmed hat on the next ranger you see here, and later if you should be at Everglades, Acadia, Mt. McKinley, or the Statute of Liberty, look again on a ranger's hat and see the same cone.

The giant sequoia of the Sierra Nevada (*Sequoiadendron giganteum* is its scientific name) is not to be confused with the Coast redwood of western California (*Sequoia sempervirens),* although it often is. The two trees grow in entirely different climates, have vastly different foliage and cones, occupy totally separate ranges, and are not even generically related, although once thought to be. The Coast redwood is the *tallest* tree on Earth, some specimens rising over 300 feet high. The giant sequoia is the *largest* tree on Earth, the Grizzly

the Wawona or Tunnel Tree – now fallen – in three phases of its last century

Giant in the Mariposa Grove for instance being 29 feet through, and weighing nearly 2 million pounds.

But the sequoias have more than spectacular appeal. They are aesthetically beautiful, too. A giant sequoia grove is a great place to let your mind drift between its modes of consciousness — the specifics imparted by the senses of seeing, feeling, smelling, hearing, tasting, and the abstractions as created in the mind. The groves have been so used for generations, and perhaps this is the tree's highest human purpose — in helping man in his intuitive and mystical quest for truth, beauty, relevance, inner meaning, or whatever the current but everchanging fashion prefers to call this aspect of the soul.

Arrive at the Mariposa Grove by way of Yosemite's South Entrance. From here, the road to the grove (3 miles) is open all year except during and after heavy winter snowstorms. Shortly after entering the grove at The Sentinels, a parking area is provided, as private cars are not permitted to drive through the grove.

Beyond, a variety of trails leads up into the two sections of the grove, and there is a tourbus for use in summer and fall. The route selected here for you connects various segments of these paths and roads, giving maximum exposure to the trees themselves. It begins at the top of the Upper Grove, descending continuously back to the parking area at the bottom of the Lower Grove.

In season, board the tourbus at the parking area and ride up to the high point of the road at the fallen Wawona or Tunnel Tree. Other times, follow up the road on foot to this point (3.4 miles and 1,020 feet of elevation gained). In winter, explore on skis or snowshoes, but be wary of the route described here as snow may cover vital directional signs or obscure pathways.

Start at the Wawona Tunnel Tree, first exploring its prostrate trunk. This sequoia tree fell in 1969 during the winter of greatest recorded snowfall for the Sierra Nevada, although it surely stood through many winters more severe before records were kept. Its 26-foot long tunnel, now collapsed, was cut in 1881 to allow stagecoaches to pass through, giving it a world fame that lasted into the era of cars and buses until its demise.

Before beginning this grove hike, you may wish to walk down the road north to the Galen Clark Tree (0.2 mile) named for the grove's explorer and first guardian, and then follow an old road leading beyond that tree up to Wawona Point (another 0.5 mile and a climb of 210 feet). From that vantage you overlook Wawona Meadow, the western Sierra slope, the South Fork of the Merced River, and the high country of southern Yosemite. By the time you return to the Tunnel Tree, you will have added about 45 minutes to the trip through the Grove.

From the fallen Tunnel Tree, proceed south up the road 0.2 mile to the Telescope Tree. As this tree's inside heartwood has been largely burned out, you can see out its top. For many years, fire was excluded from the grove, and the understory built up to conditions hazardous to the trees in the event of fire. Recently, the understory in the grove is being restored to the more

view up trunk of Telescope Tree

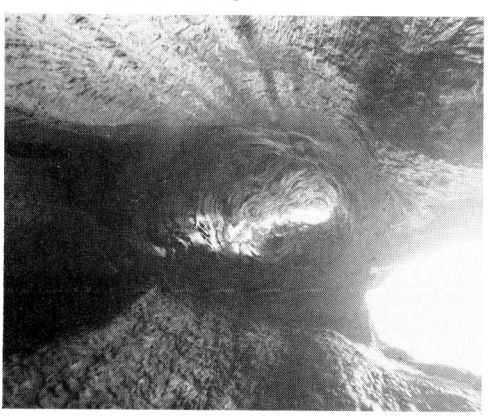

Galen Clark's cabin, now the site of the Mariposa Grove Museum.

normal open condition that prevails when natural fires run through such a forest at frequent intervals.

Turn right from the Telescope Tree downhill onto the use trail here. This leads to the Mariposa Grove Museum in 0.3 mile, passing fine mature sequoia specimens and the upturned roots of the fallen Stable Tree, in whose hollow base, while it was standing, there were once mangers. The Stable Tree fell in 1934. (If you can't find this use trail, you can also reach the Museum by continuing on the road.)

At the Museum are exhibits on the history of the sequoia and of this grove, and on the tree's ecology. Behind the Museum, a half-mile self-guiding nature trail further interprets aspects of the tree's life story. (If you wish to bypass this nature trail, proceed backwards on it from its start behind the museum, heading toward the log cabin rest rooms and then turning left onto the trail to the Lower Grove.)

The nature trail leads along one side of a meadow lined with giant trees and then crosses and comes back up the opposite side. Before returning, however, you may wish to go on 0.1 mile and cross the road to the Big Trees Lodge (now closed) to see a number of young sequoias growing before it, standing in the soil disturbed in construction, as the seedlings prefer to start life in mineral soil whether created artificially by man or naturally by fire. Their spire-like tops indicate rapid growth still. Behind the lodge are large sequoias, including the Sunset Tree, westernmost in

young giant sequoia with spire-like top

Clothespin Tree – burned through

mile to the main paved road at the Faithful Couple, their trunks joined from the ground up partway. Walk downhill along the road a short distance around the curve to the trail on the left side of the road. This leads to the Grizzly Giant. Follow this trail through a stand of sequoia-less mixed conifers until you come to more sequoias, the Lower Grove. At 0.4 mile from the Faithful Couple, our trail intersects the trail we earlier rejected above on leaving the Upper Grove where we chose the old stagecoach road instead. Now turn right here onto this trail toward the Grizzly Giant (0.2 mile). When nearly there, pass the standing California Tree, tunneled in 1895 and serv-

California Tree

the grove and hence catching the last rays of the setting sun. Its base has a fire scar 51 feet across.

Continuing around the nature trail, head back toward the Museum until the building comes in sight. The trail to the Lower Grove, which is our route, branches off to the right. We follow this trail only 0.1 mile, leaving it at the top of a slight rise where we turn right onto a wide path — an old stagecoach road — descending through the forest. Where this abandoned road forks in 0.1 mile, take the left branch heading downhill, exiting from the Upper Grove. This route is not maintained, but is generally easy to follow. There may be yellow markers high on the tree trunks along this route, indicating use as a winter trail. In 0.4 mile it reaches the main road into the grove from behind the Clothespin Tree. This sequoia is 266 feet tall. Extensive fire burns have shaped the trunk like the springless clothespin in use when it was named. Its trunk is open for 70 feet above the ground, a gap that spans 16 feet across, testimony that sequoia heartwood does burn once the thick insulating bark is breached.

Follow the trail downhill — left — 0.3

Grizzly Giant

ing until 1932 as a substitute for visitors unable because of winter snows to get into the Upper Grove and go through its Wawona Tunnel Tree. There is still one tree (or stump) you can drive through in Yosemite — the Dead Giant — in the Tuolumne Grove. Here at the California Tree you may turn right on a trail to Wawona (6.2 miles), if you have a way to travel from there, as that trail bypasses the Lower Grove parking area.

Straight beyond the tree tunnel 0.1 mile is the Grizzly Giant. It's a leaner, so consider on which side you will pass it. This is Yosemite's biggest tree and is the fifth largest of all the trees in the world! It is 2,700 years old. Various methods were tried to secure the tree against falling until it was realized that there was little man could do in propping up its 2 million pounds — at least in ways that would not harm the tree or damage its appearance. Here Nature will prevail. As this sequoia has been leaning for well over a century since before its first picture was taken, and since there has likely been compensatory root development on the side opposite the lean, the danger may not be imminent. At any rate the tree's fall is inevitable, and it will probably fall before dying as such is the fate of virtually all large sequoias.

Beyond the Grizzly Giant the trail continues downhill through the Lower Grove 0.7 mile to the parking area, crossing the paved road to the south side in 0.3 mile just above where the Bachelor and Three Graces stand. Several sequoias have fallen across the old road which is now our path. Walk around the short loop of the Lower Grove nature trail and see the Corridor Tree and other sights, ending at the parking area, where you started. You have now ridden and walked 6½ miles past some of the largest and oldest things that have ever lived. Consider your place in Nature and in Time, and don't be in too much of a rush as you leave.

Fallen Monarch

Map of Mariposa Grove

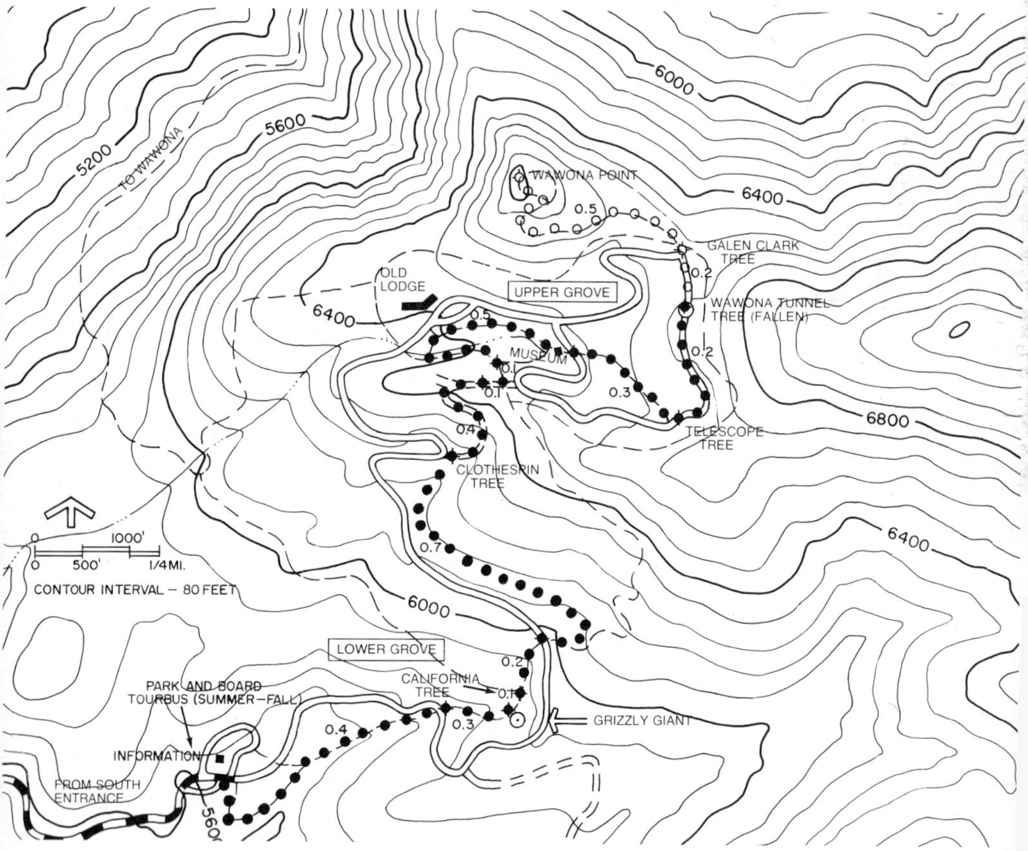

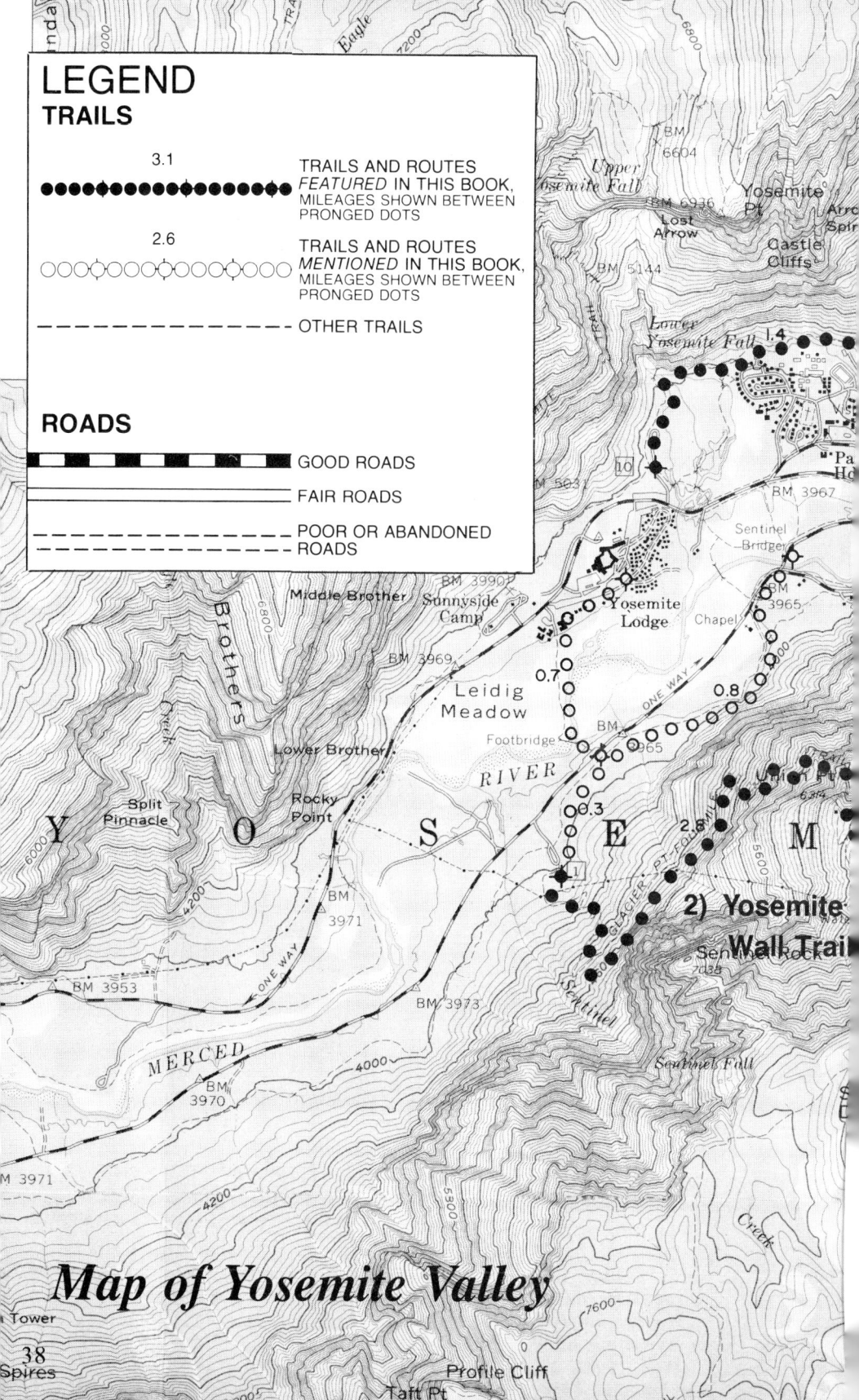

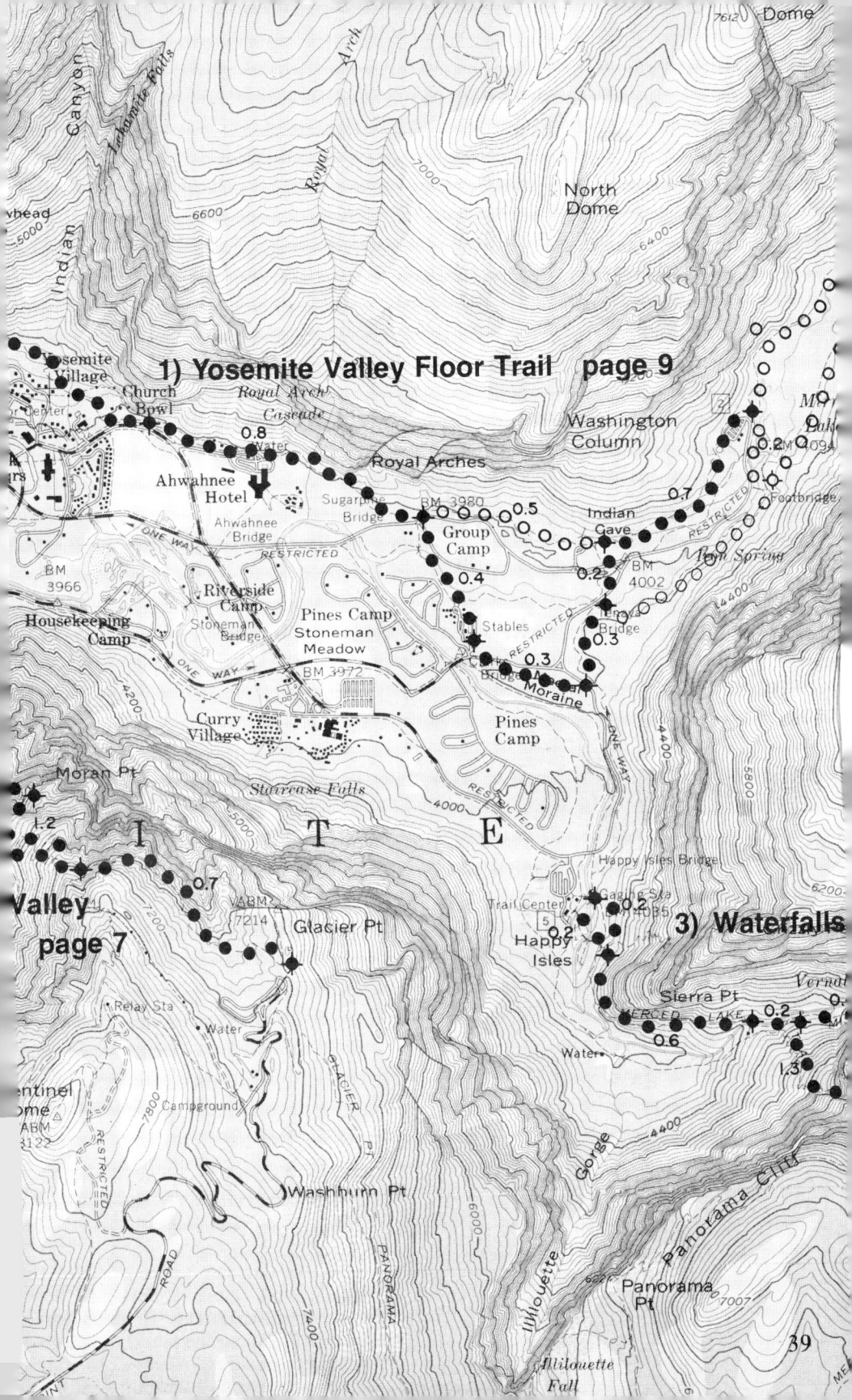

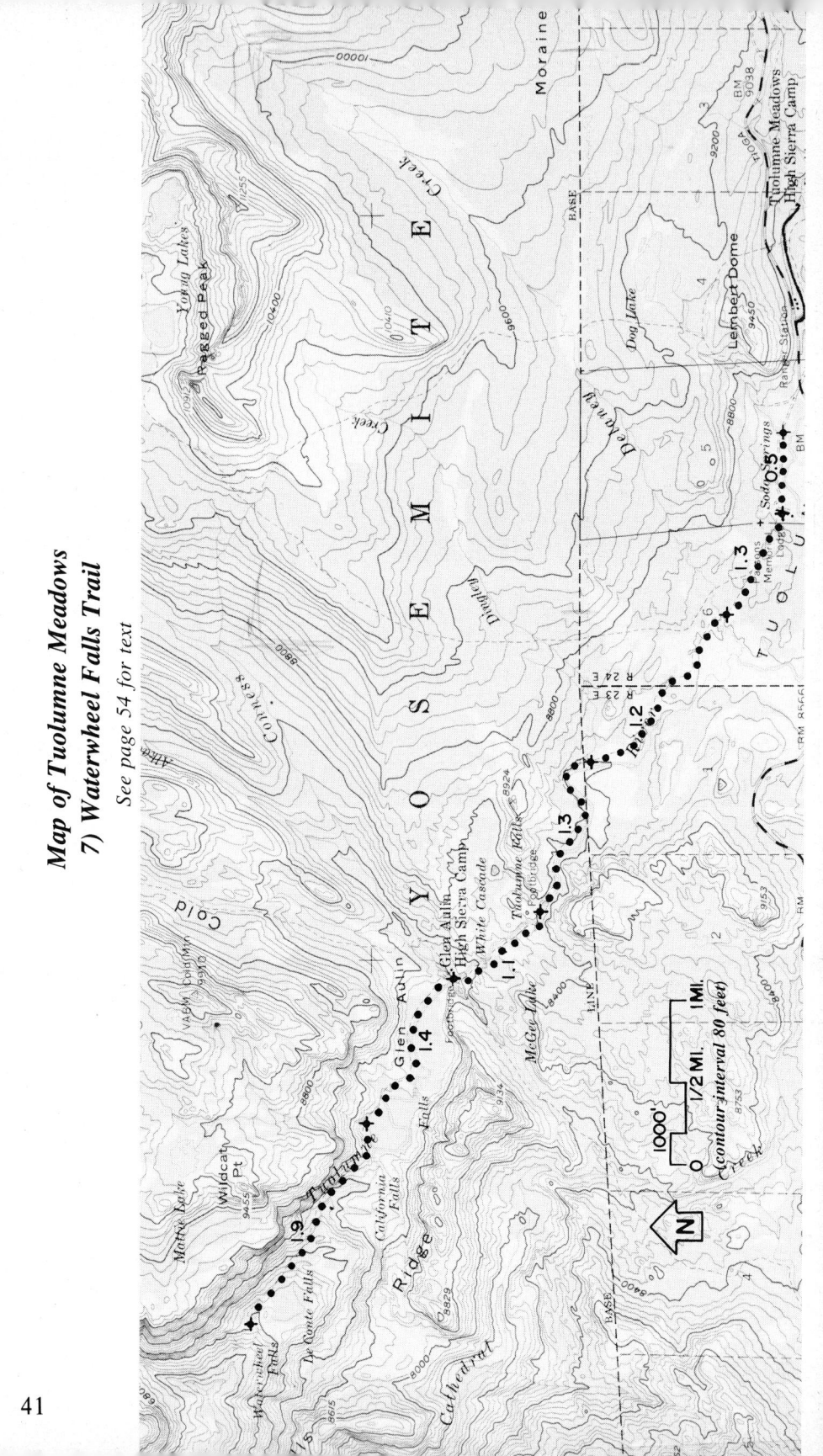

5) HIGH SIERRA
May Lake and Mount Hoffman

Start and finish: May Lake trailhead (8,850 feet) at end of spur road 1½ miles off Tioga Road

	Elevation gain, feet	Elevation loss, feet	Distance miles	Time hours
Trailhead to May Lake (9,300 feet)—one way	450	0	1.2	1½
Return from May Lake—one way	0	450	1.2	1
Round-trip totals:	450	450	2.4	2½
Trailhead to Mount Hoffman (10,850 feet)—one way	2,000	0	3.5	4
Return from Mount Hoffman—one way	0	2,000	3.5	2
Round-trip totals:	2,000	2,000	7.0	6

Seasons: All (winter and spring — sturdy cross-country skis or snowshoes needed; Tioga Road generally closed November 1 to Memorial Day in late May and spur road closed even longer).

Special notes: no trail beyond May Lake; see text for start of winter trail.

Map: page 47

Mount Hoffmann is at the center of Yosemite National Park, which means there is near-original America stretching 20 miles to its north and 20 miles to its south, as well as 15 miles to its east and to its west. It is high enough — 10,850 feet — to be just above timberline, and to have had a glacier on its north slope, head for the Yosemite Creek glacier that entered Yosemite Valley over Yosemite Falls. On the mountain's eastern slope is May Lake, a glacier-dug hollow of deep-blue waters fringed by scattered trees. Here, too, is the May Lake High Sierra Camp, part of a string of 6 backcountry tent camps where beds and

May Lake in the High Sierra below Mt. Hoffmann's eastern ridge; route to summit skirts lake on left, then heads left up low gully around this ridge to open slope and summit beyond

meals are available (with reservations well in advance of the season).

The High Sierra is not a precise term, and is used variously along the range. In Yosemite it should be reserved for lands that bear the marks of fresh glaciation, are sparsely forested or are completely open for expansive views across the smooth granite or broken rock slopes. Typical trees are the western juniper, mountain hemlock, and whitebark pine. At its lower fringe are red firs and lodgepole pines, while its upper limit extends to the mountain tops where trees are absent and only the tiny and colorful alpine plants thrive or survive. Deep snows blanket the High Sierra most of the year, and at the end of summer a long dry period is common. There are tufts of meadow grass — both on flats and on slopes — and streams lace over the bedrock with scarcely a channel. Somehow High Sierra aesthetics induce warm response in humans, and that rather than any singular feature is the region's dominant significance and greatest appeal.

You reach this trailhead via the Tioga Road, turning onto the May Lake spur at a point 26 miles east of the Crane Flat road junction, or 13 miles west of the Tuolumne Meadows Visitor Center. This winding spur lane is part of the original Tioga wagon road across the Sierra Nevada, completed in 1883 to serve mines near Tioga Pass at the range crest. On it you can get a taste of an earlier generation's travel mode, used by cars to cross the range until 1960 when replaced by the present road. En route to the trailhead, you reach Snow Flat in one mile, where a snow gauging course is maintained by park rangers in cooperation with the California Department of Water Resources. The snow, of course, is vital to the irrigation agriculture of the San Joaquin Valley far downstream. Depths here are often ten feet and more, and in the winter of 1969 the snow reached nearly twice that.

At 1.8 miles from where you left the modern Tioga Road, park at the trailhead on the left side of the spur road, just before it ends. Skirt the little pond here on the left and follow the trail, winding upward across partly open granite and forested sections (red fir and lodgepole and western white pines), reaching May Lake (9,300 feet) in 1.2 miles. This trail goes on to join the trail along the Tuolumne River at Glen Aulin.

Directly above the lake to the northwest rise the great cliffs of Mount Hoffmann's eastern ridge. This is not the summit, but at nearly the same altitude. You can stroll to the right around the lake's east and north shores to several good campsites in the mountain hemlock groves fringing the water. In fact, this stand of this tree is one of the most delightful in Yosemite. John Muir wrote of the species as "the lovely ladylike mountain hemlock," noting that its boughs

Mt. Hoffmann from the south, aerial view, showing approximate route up to summit from May Lake (out of view in lower right). Note Thumb left of summit

43

mountain hemlock at May Lake

three views east to west from Mt. Hoffmann summit:

1) Tuolumne Meadows

cloak the tree trunk clear to the ground, like ladies' skirts once did them. The tree prefers moist sites and also can grow where snow piles deep or where avalanches would break other trees, for its branches and top are limber, drooping noticeably.

The lake is open to fishing with a California license, containing eastern brook and rainbow trout, probably best late in the season. These fish were planted here, as none were left in the High Sierra after the glacier age and none could climb the waterfalls on the Snow Creek outlet stream, which tumbles into Tenaya Canyon above Yosemite Valley as Snow Creek Falls.

On the east shore is the May Lake High Sierra Camp. And on the ridge behind that is a promontory affording a fine view of the full sweep of Tenaya Canyon from Half Dome at its foot to Tenaya Lake at its head, with Cathedral Peak outlined above against the horizon. If you do not intend to go up Mount Hoffmann, where you can see much the same view but from a higher vantage, be sure to go out here.

Viewed from this ridge, a lobe of ice spilled from the left (east) over the low divide from Tuolumne Meadows, just beyond, and flowed to the right down Tenaya Canyon, filling it as high as the smoothed slopes surrounding the Cathedral Peak summit spires and three-fourths up the front of Half Dome. Only the steep hackled upper slopes of these peaks and the "comb" atop Clouds Rest stood above the sluggish white stream mass. Underneath, the ice gouged out the Lake Tenaya hollow, then flowed on down Tenaya Canyon, shaping it, to join other tributaries and carve out Yosemite Valley.

Above the left (east) end of Tenaya Lake stands high Tenaya Peak, its top also unglaciated, but with a glacial cirque scooped out of the ridge extending behind the peak itself. This "cirque" is a hollow bowl cut into the ridge, with steep cliffs and a

detail of Tenaya Peak, with cirque; locate at right center of photo number 2 above

2) Cathedral Peak, Tenaya Peak, Tenaya Lake

3) Clouds Rest, Tenaya Canyon, Half Dome, (Yosemite Valley out of view to right)

smooth lower slope at their base, the whole perched so high on the mountain that the bowl's floor is at 9,700 feet. (Cirques — the birthplaces of glaciers — did not form in Yosemite much lower than this. But the ice that accumulated in them flowed away when so deep as to squeeze the lower layers away, which then carried the upper layers with them. New snows replenished the system annually. The process spawned valley glaciers that descended to altitudes as low as 2,000 feet on the western Sierra slope.) Recently a living glacier reoccupied this cirque, reborn since the last major Ice Age pulse, but now it is gone like its predecessors. Note the fresh moraine ridge of rock rubble the vanished ice left on the floor of the hollow, at just about the point where the protecting shadow from the cliff wall behind still ends during most of the day, and outside which ice would melt rapidly.

Tenaya Lake was named for Chief Tenaya of the Yosemite Indians, on the occasion of the tribe's final capture on its shores — May 22, 1851. The chief protested, however, saying the lake already had a name — "Pywiack, the lake of the shining rocks."

An earlier generation also came out to this ridge for the view, with one added attraction at night. They could watch the Firefall for the moment or so it lasted. This was a dry cascade of glowing embers made from the bark of the red fir tree and pushed off Glacier Point to drop into Yosemite Valley and awe the tourists there. (The cliff used, far to the southwest from here and across the valley on the opposite wall, can still be recognized by the light-colored vertical band down its center, showing where the darker lichen growths were burned off the lighter gray granite underneath. It is just left — east — of Sentinel Dome, the light-colored rock bulge in the forest near the horizon.)

Mount Hoffmann is a 2-mile hike beyond May Lake, with 1,500 feet more of climbing. It is not a technical mountain climb, but as there is no formal trail, it does require simple route finding, and it is strenuous. Nevertheless, most will successfully complete the trip unless they are distracted along the way. And well they might be, for John Muir found that "On no other Yosemite Park mountain are you more likely to

phlox

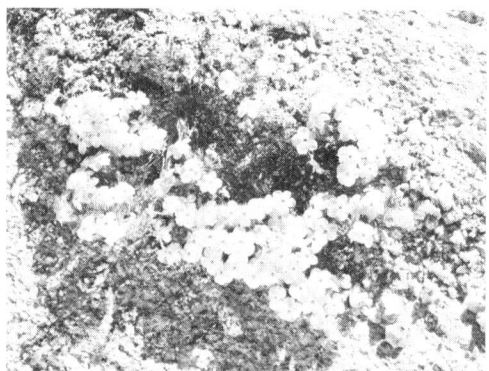

Mt. Hoffmann summit with Thumb

linger.... You saunter among the crystals and flowers as if you were walking among stars." So add some time for enjoyment. In midsummer over 100 varieties of wildflowers can be counted on Mount Hoffmann and its neighboring slopes, and you should make the effort of getting to know some of them, especially if you brought along a book on alpine plants.

The first ascent was made by Josiah Dwight Whitney, William H. Brewer, and Charles F. Hoffmann (the mountain's namesake), as part of their work with the California Geological Survey, on June 24, 1863.

The cliffs above the lake are the eastern end of the summit ridge of the mountain. The summit itself is a quarter-mile behind that, beyond a dip in the ridge, and only slightly higher. Our route swings to the left, south and then west, around these cliffs, and upward.

Walk along the southern shore of the lake (the left shore as you looked at Mount Hoffmann from the trail where you first approached the lake), passing some more campsites and crossing the lake's Snow Creek outlet stream. Watch here at any season for blue grouse — a large poor-flying bird that feeds on the most abundant food hereabout — evergreen tree needles. A band of red-and-gray partly-layered metamorphic rocks is crossed here. Just before reaching the cliff wall on the western shore, turn left (south) and walk up the path in the floor of the gully there, holding this same course for the next half-mile. Rock cairns or ducks (artificially stacked boulders) may be helpful in finding the route but some may lead astray.

Soon the top of the gully is reached, and the elongate level meadow there. At the meadow's far end, cross it and head left gradually up the slope on a path that is faint to plain, then turn up the slope more directly for the mountain. From this point up, if not already, you may see the tiny pika — or hear its high-pitched squeal. These little rock rabbits (also called conies) cut grass from meadow patches tucked among the rocks, cure it to hay in the sun, and then store it in piles under the rocks to eat in winter when snow blankets the ground, as they do not hibernate.

This is Yosemite timberline country — home of the whitebark pine, a 5-needled tree, and the Clark's nutcracker, a large gray-and-white bird that feeds on the nuts in the pine's cones. Continue ascending the slope above, heading generally just left (west) around the cliffs you saw above May Lake, then more northerly toward the saddle between these cliffs and the summit farther on the left (west). At the saddle, turn left (due west) and scramble upward over scattered loose boulders and steep granite slabs to the top. You will be watched by marmots, or "rockchucks", as you pass by their homes under the boulders. A register is usually at the summit, and a radio antenna for the park ranger network.

view north from Mt. Hoffmann summit

From here you see 1,000 feet down the northern mountain wall into the horseshoe-shaped head of Yosemite Creek, with its numerous little meadow- or rock-bordered glacier-scooped lakelets. These, along with deep snowbanks in the shadows, form the main source of Yosemite Creek — which starts out here northwesterly, then swings to the south toward Yosemite Valley, dropping in as Yosemite Falls.

Stretching north beyond the lakelets you may notice a lighter-colored band of rock. This is marble, a metamorphosed limestone deposit left from when an ancient sea covered this area. These ancient rocks of calcium carbonate, formerly shells of minute sea animals, often became the sites where unusual minerals were later deposited, frequently economically valuable varieties. Such was the case here, and in 1881 silver was found and the Mount Hoffmann Mining District was organized. This was perfectly legal, for at the time the park had not been established. The district amounted to nothing, however — fortunately for the High Sierra here. A few small caves also occur in the marble, for water dissolves this rock.

cony

Just south of our peak is the Hoffmann Thumb, a pinnacle of horizontally-fractured rock standing as the high point of a similar-appearing ridge. It was first

Map of Tenaya Lake-Mt. Hoffmann

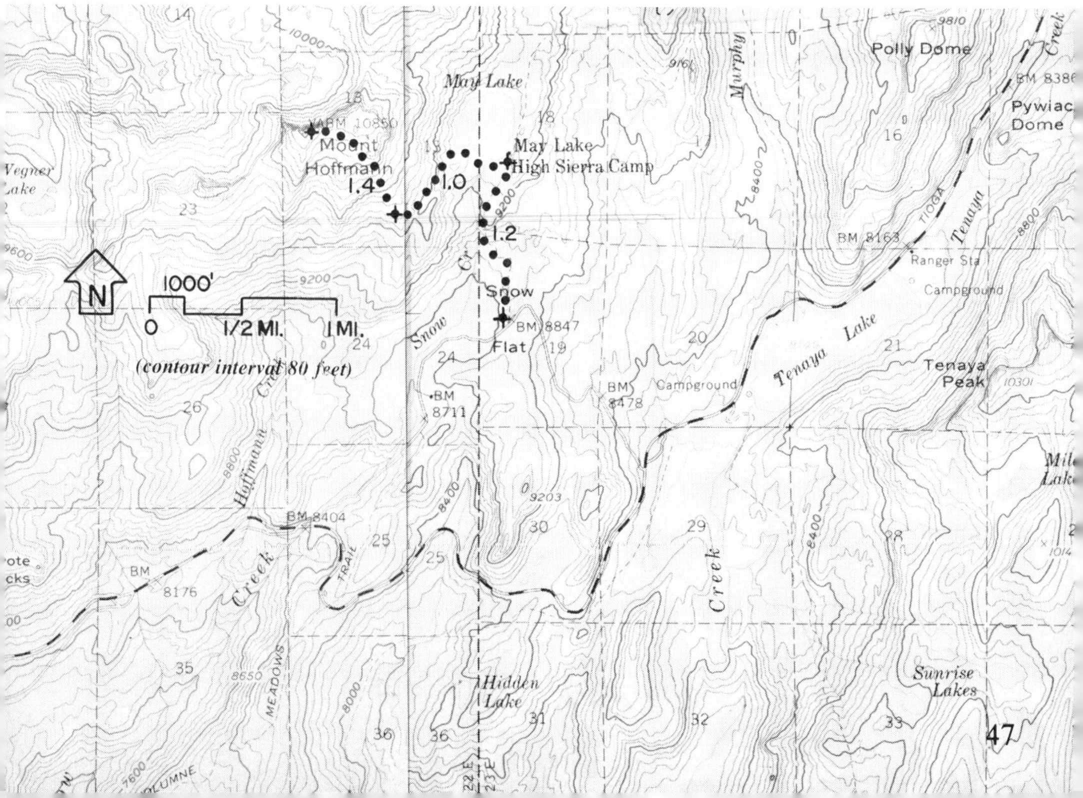

climbed in 1932, and is obviously technical. Note this distinctive feature, for it identifies Mount Hoffmann from virtually every high point in the southern half of the park. Stretching beyond is the same panorama seen from the ridge east of May Lake and described earlier (although the view is higher and better toward Yosemite Valley). You can also see to the west slope of the Sierra, and to the southern edge of the Merced River drainage on the Horse Ridge-Buena Vista Crest horizon.

Climb down from the summit the same way you came up, enjoy the view down the north wall from the slot at the saddle, and then walk up toward the middle false summit. Partway there, turn around and see the impressively vertical north side of Hoffmann, where you were just perched. Continue around the left side of the central outcrop, an easy walk on this smoother summit area, to the two prominent outcroppings beyond. Between them, view May Lake below, where you stood earlier.

Return to May Lake by any of the open routes that seems most appealing (remembering the locations of cliffs below you, however), and then follow back to the spur road on the trail you used earlier.

In winter and spring (as late as May or early June most years), the Mount Hoffmann trip can be made on skis or snowshoes. If the Tioga Road is open but the May Lake spur is still closed, the easiest route starts from the main road and follows a ridge up to Snow Flat. Drive up the Tioga Road to a point 0.6 mile east of the May Lake spur road turnoff and park just east of the ridgecrest. This ridge is the top of a glacial moraine of loose boulder and fine rock debris, which may however at this time be blanketed with snow. Look here for brightly-colored metal markers, often painted license plates, high on the tree trunks. The ones you want are northeast of the road; they lead up the ridge to Snow Flat, where they end. (The others southwest of the road lead down the ridge and Snow Creek to the top of the Tenaya Zigzags on the trail to Mirror Lake in Yosemite Valley, the approach if the Tioga Road is closed.)

From Snow Flat, follow the Old Tioga Road to the summer trailhead described earlier and proceed the same way to the lake or the mountain, but with route finding and with no trail all the way. A winter ascent up the south bowl of the mountain can also be made from Snow Flat, but the approach is rough and there is avalanche hazard on that route at times, especially during and following snowstorms or in springs of heavy snow years.

Just such trips as these marked the start of early ski activities in the park and in the Sierra, in the 1920s. Then lodging, meals, and instruction were provided in cabins based at May Lake and on the west slope of the Mount Watkins ridge between here and Yosemite Valley! Now interest in this since-ignored activity has revived, and thousands of ski touring parties go out into the park every winter. The Hoffmann trip, however, should not be your first winter one, nor should the one to May Lake be, as these are ski mountaineering rather than touring. See the description of the Ostrander Hut Ski Trail, for those less experienced, if in doubt, perhaps considering a half-day trip from Badger Pass in to Bridalveil Creek Campground for your first venture off the practice slopes.

cross-country skiers

6) *GLACIAL LANDSCAPE*
Tuolumne Meadows-Lembert Dome

Start and Finish: Dog Lake Trailhead parking area (8,600 feet) at western base of Lembert Dome

	Elevation gain, feet	Elevation loss, feet	Distance miles	Time hours
One-way to top of Lembert Dome (9,450 feet)	850	0	1.2	1½ - 2
One-way return	0	850	2.0	1
Round-trip totals:	850	850	3.2	3

Seasons: all (winter and spring — cross-country skis or snowshoes needed and possibly crampons and ice axe for summit, with potential for avalanche; Tioga Road generally closed November 1 to Memorial Day in late May).

Map: page 53

Lembert Dome in Tuolumne Meadows

John Muir called Tuolumne "the most delightful summer pleasure-park in all the High Sierra." Then as now it was also the most accessible, serving as a trail hub to the finest of mountain rambles. Muir advised "a whole month, or even two months, will not be too long for this grand High Sierra excursion." (His own Sierra trip was ten years long, he said.)

Muir's description of the Meadows — wide, smooth, and serenely spacious — is poetic:

"Down through the open sunny meadow-levels flows the Tuolumne River, fresh and cool from its many glacial fountains. . . . Narrow strips of pine woods cross the meadow-carpet from side to side, and it is somewhat roughened here and there by moraine boulders . . . but for miles and miles it is so smooth and level that a hundred horsemen may ride abreast over it."

Muir spent the summer of 1869 at Tuolumne, assisting in the tending of a flock of sheep but with an arrangement that allowed him plenty of time for exploring. Muir might now be criticized for being so employed, as sheep are hard on mountain meadows and overgrazing later became rampant, one reliable observer (Professor Joseph LeConte) counting 25,000 head in the area. To Muir's credit, however, he later condemned the animals as "hoofed locusts" and years later around a campfire at Tuolumne he and his publisher launched the effort to establish Yosemite National Park, realized in 1890. This was none too soon, for an 1891 government engineering report showed in detail how the Meadows might be flooded by a dam at the western outlet. These and other threats to national parks inspired formation of the Sierra Club, with Muir as first president. To marshal support for conserving Yosemite, high trips were organized, many emanating from a base in Tuolumne Meadows at Soda Springs. And so Tuolumne has become a part of the Club's traditions and heritage, and remains a favorite with members. Of

Tuolumne Meadows in 1867. Note large angled rock and tree in center of meadow. River goes to left around these; no trees on foreground rocks

Tuolumne Meadows in 1976. Note large angled rock and tree still in center of meadow. But now river goes to right in front of these; trees have grown on foreground rocks.

course, hundreds of thousands of others came to know and love the area, too.

Tuolumne Meadows exists because it was glaciated. Ice flowed down from cirque-hollows on the surrounding peaks and clogged the entire basin, filling it to a depth of 2,200 feet. Because the basin is so broad, the ice was not channeled, and erosion was not great, yet all the soil was scraped away and the bare bedrock gouged. When the ice melted, it left an undulating surface with bosses of tougher granite swelling up amid water-filled troughs. The scene was between an island-studded lake and a pond-pocked granite floor, the whole scattered with loose glacial debris. In the 10,000 or so years since then, the Tuolumne River and its side streams joining it in the Meadows have largely filled in the hollows with silt and these have coalesced to form an almost continuous soil mantle supporting grasses and sedges; but a few open ponds remain, especially in the western end farthest away from the entering silt load.

Old photos show fewer trees than now and more rocks. The sod is "swallowing" the boulders as it builds and the trees come out from the forest as seedlings when the soil stands high enough to provide some air above the water table for roots. Lodgepole pine is more tolerant of such conditions than other native trees and enters along the meadow fringe and by following out along old roads and trails where the turf was once broken. High meadows are ecologically fragile and if disturbed may change to a new condition rather than reheal to the previous state.

In the midst of the forest and meadow-carpet, Lembert Dome rises island-like, itself only a larger bump on the glacier's old bed. From its summit in all directions is a fantastic panorama of a glacial landscape, *the* place to get oriented to the region and its glacial history.

Start for the top from the Dog Lake/Young Lakes trailhead 0.1 mile east of the Tuolumne River bridge. This is on the north side of the Tioga Road, right at the western base of the dome itself. Walk northwest on the Dog Lake Trail 100 yards,

lodgepole pines invading Tuolumne Meadows along an abandoned trail

showing ledges   *detail of "mountaineer's friend" feldspar crystal*

Cathedral Peak granite on route to summit of Lembert Dome

then turn right (northeast) onto a faint old road that soon crosses a bare granite area, leading 250 yards more up to a large radio building nestled in the trees under the dome. There are severl other paths to this point also. The use trail from here is plain in most places; it climbs steeply through the woods. The many branches usually recombine; use the map to be sure you stay generally on course, however. Most of the trees are lodgepole pines, but you will also come to mountain hemlocks and western white pines.

After passing under the dome's northeastern slope of bare rock, passing a few openings in the forest, the use trail begins ascending through a finger of trees that leads between the main dome and its small cousin dome just north of this path. At the use-trail's crest (1.0 mile from our start), the open rock of the dome summit slopes upward to the right. Follow this granite ridge 0.2 mile to the top, finding your own route upward over the granite ledges, passing whitebark pines and glacial erratics. Soon you will see the summit, atop a little cone of steeper rock. Head for the left side of this, then follow back toward the summit along a weak fracture zone where the rock has more ledges and places to hold. You will use your hands a few times, a sort of mini-rock climb, but the ascent is well within the capabilities of almost all. Experiment with the friction of your shoe soles where it is safe in order to learn on what slopes they will hold you. Use the large feldspar crystals — "mountaineer's friends" — that often protrude from this rock (the Cathedral Peak granite) to gain purchase, and soon you're on the top, which is capped by a glacial boulder.

South, you can see up the Lyell Canyon clear to Lyell Glacier, glistening in the sun even in late summer. Mounts Dana and Gibbs are the reddish mountains on the east at the range crest, made of metamorphic rock rather than granite as is Lembert Dome. Northeast over Dog Lake (in the forest below; use map) is high Mount Conness. Looking west you see almost the whole of Tuolumne Meadows, with the river draining through it toward the outlet on the right — headed for Waterwheel Falls, the Grand Canyon of the Tuolumne River, Hetch Hetchy Valley, and, in part, by pipeline to San Francisco. Domes at that end of the Meadows have rounded backs and shoulders facing not only us but

Lembert Dome summit, showing approximate route

also the glacier fountains of the summit mountains, the same as has Lembert Dome. The downstream fronts of these same domes, split and angular, drop off sharply, also like Lembert's face (the cliff we now stand above). This "lop-sided" configuration reveals the tremendous grinding force with which the ice-flood passed over them, and also shows the direction of its flow, for the glacier would have trimmed away or smoothed down any cliff standing to oppose its current.

On the southwestern skyline are Cathedral Peak, Echo Peaks, Unicorn Peak, and others that have steep hackly upper slopes and smooth lower ones. The line between their upper and lower slopes is called the schrund line. Above this, when the glacier was present, meltwater seeped into cracks on the cliff face and refroze there, dislodging blocks of rock. Below this schrund line, the ice flowed away, carrying off the broken rocks and rounding and polishing the bedrock underneath. There was so much ice coming into the Meadows area that it could not get out immediately, and so piled up. Most of it went down the Tuolumne River outlet clear to Hetch Hetchy Valley, generating a glacier sixty miles long — the longest ever in the Sierra. But much ice also flowed up over the low divide now crossed by the Tioga Road entering the Meadows from the west. This latter ice stream passed Tenaya Lake and went on down Tenaya Canyon to Yosemite Valley, sculpting Half Dome on the way.

More direct proof of the glacier is at hand right on Lembert Dome. You may have noticed loose dark-colored rocks different from the Dome's crystal-laden "Cathedral Peak granite" bedrock. These darker boulders came from the metamorphic rocks that occur farther east, perhaps even from Mount Lyell where similar rocks occur. There are also patches of glacial polish, and scratches on that showing the direction of flow. At the Ice Age maximum, our perch (nearly 1,000 feet above Tuolumne Meadows) was itself under more than 1,000 feet of ice!

Scout your next hikes from here. Will you go up Mount Dana (east)? The route begins left of the mountain, at Tioga Pass (out of sight behind a ridge), and climbs upward to the right near the skyline. Mount Lyell (south) is a long walk up the level-floored Lyell Canyon (angling left, then due south) and then a steep ascent to the peak. Waterwheel Falls (northwest) is down the Tuolumne River farther than you can see. Mount Hoffman is off to the west, beyond Tuolumne Peak. These hikes are described in this guide, and there are many more from Tuolumne — Elizabeth Lake, Dog and Young Lakes, Vogelsang, and on and on. Cross-country routefinders can find Cathedral Cirque and the Kuna Crest. Mountaineers can climb Fairview Dome and The Unicorn — from "easy" (for them) or difficult sides.

Now explore Lembert Dome. A good viewpoint is another 0.2 mile farther out to the west beyond the summit, but don't continue too far that way for the slope steepens to a rock climb. Also, the southern slopes of the dome are gouged by deep and irregular channels.

When you have had your fill of the scene, retrace your steps back northeast along the dome's ridgecrest to the forest.

Tuolumne Meadows from summit Lembert Dome; Cathedral Peak on left skyline

Mt. Lyell and Lyell Glacier from summit Lembert Dome

There you can turn left onto the use trail you came up and go directly back to the dome's western base if you wish. That is the faster and shorter way back. The return described here, however, continues ahead straight off the dome's ridge through the forest, dropping gradually 0.3 mile to the maintained Dog Lake/Young Lake Trail. (This is not the same Dog Lake/Young Lake Trail you saw earlier at the western base of Lembert Dome; this one starts at the dome's eastern base, meeting the other to the north of Lembert Dome.) Turn right (south) on this maintained trail and drop another 0.4 mile back to the Tioga Road. Cross the road and soon leave the trail, headed right toward an obvious large parking area below. Beyond that, cross another road (the Old Tioga Road) to its south side and turn right (west) on the trail leading downstream along the north side of the Dana Fork of the Tuolumne River. The stream has inviting little rapids, and you continue through a lodgepole forest with meadow openings. The Tuolumne Meadows Ranger Station, passed 0.3 mile after crossing to this south side of the Old Tioga Road, sits north of the largest of the meadows, and at the far west end of that meadow Puppy Dome stands on the left (south) of the trail. This is a glacially sculpted *roche moutonnee* the same as Lembert Dome, and has a similar configuration — smoothed upstream slope and steep downstream dropoff. You can easily scramble up the back side for good views, especially at sunset, or up the right front to a ledge midway up.

Here, as at most places about Tuolumne Meadows, the trees are lodgepole pines. These trees have fairly short needles, in bundles of two, and small cones. Their bark is rather thin, even at maturity, and so takes carvings well. Look for some (don't leave any of your own) and you may find the one at the west end of the meadow by Puppy Dome, on the left side of the trail. The inscription carries a date of July 1903.

In wet spots of this meadow and the next, you'll find (in season) purple-flowered and long-stemmed wild onions. The Dana Fork joins the Lyell Fork of the Tuolumne River in the next big opening in the woods, with the campground across the river from here. Following the trail, continue to the western base of Lembert Dome, crossing the new Tioga Road to the parking area and your starting point.

Map of Lembert Dome trail

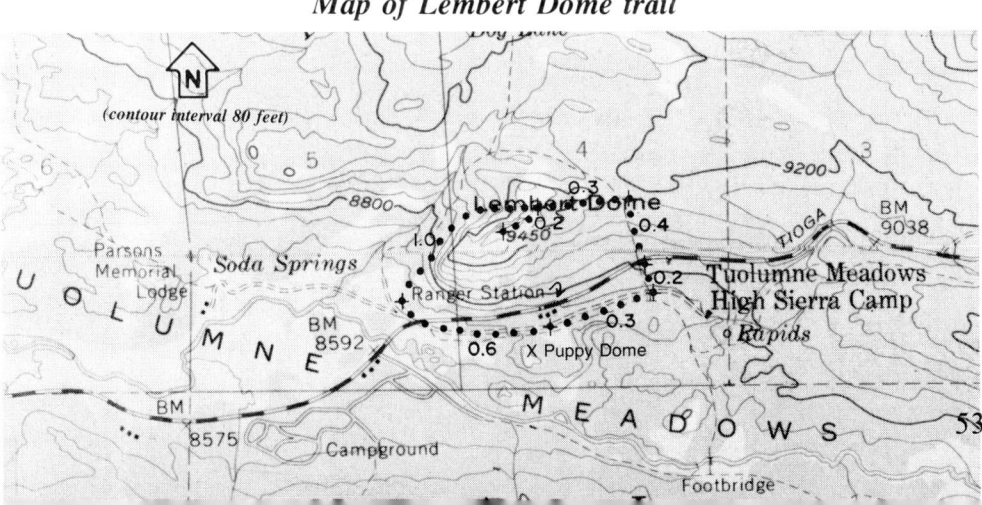

7) YOSEMITE WILDERNESS
Tuolumne River to Waterwheel Falls

Start and Finish: Soda Springs/Glen Aulin trailhead (8,590 feet), at end of spur road 0.3 mile off Tioga Road, in Tuolumne Meadows. (Parking also available at base of Lembert Dome 0.3 mile east and at wilderness permit station 0.4 mile up Tioga Road from there.)

	Elevation gain, feet	Elevation loss, feet	Distance miles	Time hours
One-way Soda Springs to Glen Aulin (7,900 feet)	40	340	5.2	3
One-way return from Glen Aulin	340	40	5.2	3
Round-trip totals:	380	380	10.4	6
One-way Soda Springs to Waterwheel Falls (6,760 feet)	40	1,860	8.7	5
One-way return from Waterwheel Falls	1,860	40	8.7	7
Round-trip totals:	1,900	1,900	17.4	2 days

Seasons: summer and fall
Map: Centerfold, page 41

Glen Aulin

For miles below Tuolumne Meadows, the Tuolumne River slips and slides and rolls down gently inclined granite slabs, through trench-slots, and past verdant meadows. Deer frequent the region; the

Tuolumne River valley between Tuolumne Meadows (upper left) and Glen Aulin; aerial; approximate trail route shown

Tuolumne River and Meadows

lodgepole pine forest is nearly pure; and glacial markings abound. Indeed, the longest glacier of the Sierra followed this same course. The moving ice created and then left the rock and waterfall features we see today; the streams and rains in many places have not since worn them away even a tenth of an inch.

Here, too, is Yosemite wilderness, much as it was in 1833 when the first of modern men saw it (the Walker party). It is now intended to stay as it is. Even natural tree-killers are left alone; needleminer moths undisturbedly continue to eat out their tiny homes in the needles of the lodgepole pines, eventually killing the mature trees, which next become woodpecker homes, then ant, grub, and bee nests which are later torn apart by a wandering bear to eventually succumb in a stomach. Here, as untrammeled as ecology can be kept, are natural species on their land — for research, for intrigue, and for their own sakes — as man need not dominate, judge, or affect everything on Earth. This trail has great appeal along its entire length, so you can go as far as you like and still reap rewards. If you go beyond Glen Aulin, however, you will probably want to stay out overnight. You can sleep in a bed and eat cooked meals at Glen Aulin High Sierra Camp (with reservations well in advance of the season) or you can backpack to several sites along the river, with a wilderness permit.

Start this trip at Tuolumne Meadows. Turn northwest off the Tioga Road at the base of Lembert Dome, at a point 0.1 mile east of the bridge over the Tuolumne River.

Drive along this lane 0.3 mile toward Soda Springs to a road gate. (Note that the small soda springs near this gate are not the main Soda Springs.) Park here or drive on to the nearby stables parking area, just up the hill to the right (north). (Parking is also available at the base of Lembert Dome 0.3 mile east and at the wilderness permit station 0.4 mile further east yet up the Tioga Road.)

Walk along the road past the gate a half mile to Soda Springs, nearer the Tuolumne River. Follow the Glen Aulin Trail. At Soda Springs you can drink the bitter natural soda water as it bubbles from the ground. Mileages from this point are 4.7 miles to Glen Aulin High Sierra Camp, 5.3 to Glen Aulin, and 8.2 to Waterwheel Falls. Pass to the right of the springs and adjacent Parsons Memorial Lodge, following the trail up the gentle slope, soon entering lodgepole pine woods. Rarely, chips of obsidian, a glassy black volcanic rock not native to Yosemite, may be seen in the light-colored granite sand off the trail. These are flakes broken off by Indians in the process of making arrowheads, acquired probably by barter from the Mono people to the east. Where most common, they often indicate locations of former Indian camps.

Cross Delaney Creek (no bridge). Soon the trail to Young Lakes (4.7 miles) branches to the right (north). From here Glen Aulin is 4.0 miles and Waterwheel Falls is 6.9 miles.

For the first few miles the trail stays back

Unicorn Peak from Soda Springs, Tuolumne Meadows

Tuolumne Cascades, below Tuolumne Meadows

in the forest from the river, but as it generally trends in the same direction as the stream, you can go over to it where it leaves the Meadows a little beyond a mile from Soda Springs and walk along its many delightful pools and cascades. This is a rougher route than the trail but still relatively easy for cross-country, and to most will be well worth the extra effort and time. Apparently the hiking enthusiast John Muir thought so, too, writing about this trip:

> "It is better to go leisurely, prepared to camp anywhere, and enjoy the marvelous grandeur of the place. . . . It is the cascades or sloping falls on the main river that are the crowning glory of the canyon, and these in volume, extent and variety surpass those of any other canyon in the Sierra. The most showy and interesting of them are mostly in the upper part of the canyon. . . . For miles the river is one wild, exulting, on-rushing mass of snowy purple bloom, spreading over glacial waves of granite without any definite channel, gliding in magnificent silver plumes, dashing and foaming through huge boulder-dams, leaping high into the air in wheel-like whirls, displaying glorious enthusiasm, singing in exuberance of mountain energy. . . . Every one who is anything of a mountaineer should go through the entire length of the canyon. . . . There is not a dull step all the way. With wide variations, it is a Yosemite Valley from end to end."

By now you have dropped below the main Tuolumne Meadows and the trail (if you are on it) swings close to the River, soon crossing Dingley Creek.

If you are going cross-country you will eventually recross the trail or can get to it by bearing right (east) through the woods away from the river.

At a point about 3½ miles below Soda Springs, the trail is on a granite rock outcrop a bit above the river, and just across the channel is a darker rock separated into vertical columns. This is the "Little Devils Postpile", a volcanic intrusion into the Cathedral Peak granite that is 9.5 million years old (whereas the granite here and around it is some 80 million years old). This postpile is named for its more famous and bigger cousin just south of Yosemite on the eastern side of the Sierra near Mammoth at Devils Postpile National Monument. Note here the lighter colored boulders lying loose on the top of the formation. These are blocks of granite, dropped there by the last glacier that went by, perhaps "only" 10,000 years ago, and are called "glacial erratics" as they seem out of place. (Good cross-country hikers can also get to this postpile along the opposite southwestern side of the River by a variety of pleasant routes past domes, ponds, meadows, pools, and cascades by beginning at the west end of Tuolumne Meadows.) Just below the postpile (3.6 miles below Soda Springs), the trail crosses the river to the southwest bank on bridges and it is also

"T" tree blaze

White Cascade

easy to return from there upstream on that shore for a closer look at the dark rock, or with extra effort and skill to return to the Meadows, especially if a car was left along the Tioga Road at one of the parking turnouts at the western end.

Tuolumne Falls and White Cascade are passed. In 1.1 miles below the last bridge, pass the junction with the McGee Lake Trail and just beyond cross the Tuolumne River again on another bridge. On the northeast bank now, to reach the Glen Aulin High Sierra Camp, turn right on the trail and walk up the Tuolumne River 0.1 mile, crossing the tributary Conness Creek. To continue toward Glen Aulin itself and Waterwheel Falls (3.3 miles from here), take the left trail branch. A third trail goes up Cold Canyon.

For the next mile the trail down the river is nearly level through the placid stretch of Glen Aulin, a filled-in glacial lake basin, with evergreen and aspen stands (bright yellow in autumn) and good campsites. Beaver signs have been noted here, quite odd in Yosemite's High Sierra, for the species is not definitely known as native to the park.

Now the drops begin. California Falls is 1.5 miles below the lower end of Glen Aulin, and LeConte Falls 0.7 mile more. Be sure to go on another 0.6 mile as far as Waterwheel Falls, really a long and steep cascade, and see its spectacular cartwheeling water arcs thrown into the air as high as 30 to 40 feet by obstructions in the granite stream floor. July is usually best for this action. Too soon and high water volume smothers the plumes. Too late and the wheels are thin. Still, the falls fascinate all these times. The slope is steep and people have slid down it, so get your drink and take your picture carefully; the rock near the water has been polished slick by both glacier and water, it will be even more slippery where wet, and it could have loose sand grains or pine needles on it.

Your return is along the same route followed on the way in, with more sidetrips possible — up the Cold Canyon trail above Glen Aulin, or southwest to McGee Lake, 0.8 mile from where you last crossed the main River near Glen Aulin. You can also make the sorties out to the River from the main trail you might have missed on the way in, or follow the River on either bank (if the water is low enough to cross) from the Little Devils Postpile clear back to Tuolumne Meadows and walk through them, possibly noting the buck deer herd, fawns, or wildflowers in season on the way back to Soda Springs. (Note that you must be on the north bank before reaching the Meadows and that a walk through them won't work in early summer until the annual flood subsides and the level areas begin to dry.) The river — with its rippling currents, sand bars, and trout to peer at — and the Tuolumne Peaks standing all about, will be there for you, too.

Waterwheel Falls

8) SIERRA CREST
Mount Dana

Start and Finish: Tioga Pass (9,945 feet)

	Elevation gain, feet	Elevation loss, feet	Distance miles	Time hours
One-way to top of Mount Dana (13,053 feet)	3,108	0	3.0	5
One-way return from top	0	3,108	3.0	3
Round-trip totals:	3,108	3,108	6.0	8

Seasons: all (winter and spring — mountaineering skis or snowshoes and crampons needed, possibility then of avalanche; Tioga Road generally closed November 1 to Memorial Day in late May).

Notes: no maintained trail, altitude effects (shortness of breath, nausea) likely. Consider carrying water, warm clothing for summit, raingear.

Map: page 63

Here is the crest of the Sierra Nevada, of some 400 miles extent north and south — the long gentle western slope here stretching 70 miles down to the San Joaquin Valley, and the eastern escarpment dropping steeply through Lee Vining Canyon to the Mono Lake plain less than 6 miles away. Water falling on the west side of this pass eventually quenches San Francisco thirst,

Mt. Dana, showing approximate route

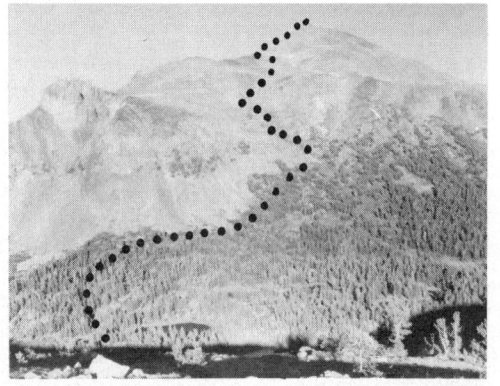

Mt. Dana from Tioga Pass, with use trail defined by a path

while that landing on the east side goes the opposite path to finally reach Los Angeles.

It wasn't always so. Tioga Pass is one of a series in this region — others being Mono Pass, Parker Pass, possibly Donohue Pass, and Minaret Summit — that were formerly parts of stream valleys that originated varying distances to the east, some perhaps even in Nevada. These valleys drained waters from that territory all during the time it and the Sierra Nevada were warping upward. Giant sequoia trees, now known in Nevada only as fossils, probably migrated along these streams during climatic fluctuations, some coming to their present western Sierra locations.

Then some of these valleys began to founder in their eastern sections. Concurrently the Ice Age began. Glaciers coursed along these drainages. One flowed through Tioga Pass and past Mount Dana. Finally, the earth began to break in a tremendous but discontinuous series of fractures along what was to become the eastern front of the Sierra. Continuous ridges of moraine deposits as regular as railroad embankments, left by the earliest ice tongues on the sides of these valleys, were subsequently offset at the fault line, their eastern portions being dropped thousands of feet. Even the similar deposits left by the most recent glaciers show the same kind of offset, although of much less magnitude because most of the faulting was completed before these more modern ridges were created. Earthquakes still shake this part of the range. In 1872, California's greatest earthquake was along this line to the south, and in 1975 one was centered close to here near the town of Lee Vining.

Standing above the pass on the east is Mount Dana. The prominent butte partway up is Lion's Head, also called Lying Head (apparently for its profile from farther west). Its top stood above the glaciers. Sedimentary and volcanic layers show in it and in the upper part of the Dana peak above. These strata are much younger than most of the similar rock in the range and hence, having passed through fewer periods of stress, are thus less highly flexed and not as hard. They have colors of chocolate brown, cream, and red, while up close the pale green mineral epidote shows abundantly. These and the still-older rocks were both intruded by the lighter-colored granites more typical of Yosemite, when the granites were in a hot and molten state. This intrusion changed the appearance of all the earlier rocks from the originally deposited material, giving them their name "metamorphic" rocks.

Perhaps of greater interest is the comparative smoothness of the western slopes of upper Mount Dana and others at the crest of the Sierra. These were never glaciated, standing so high above the glaciers in the valleys below that they still reflect the shape of the land before the Ice Age. Yet on the eastern sides of many of these same peaks, steep cliffs drop down into bowls that contain ice today. The snow collected where the shadows were, and those darker areas became the sites where the glaciers formed, and then eroded into their harboring slopes, making for themselves taller cliffs with even longer shadows. The same situation was repeated all along the Sierra crest, so that asymmetric peaks (like Dana) are typical.

Timberline is plain on the slopes of Mount Dana — at about 10,600 feet. On the side fronting Tioga Pass, avalanche tracks can be seen passing through the forest, giving visible warning to winter travelers. Although seeming a desert above, life does not stop at timberline. Alpine plants, some with as many petals as leaves, thrive clear to the top of Dana. They are isolated there, unable to propagate downward through other plant belts and spread, yet many of these species occur throughout the world. How? During the Ice Age advances of glaciers, colder and wetter climates on the land allowed arctic plants to move far south, and also allowed the alpine plants on peaktops to descend to the plains and mingle with the newly arrived arctics. When the weather warmed, all were forced to again move to favorable sites. Both the alpines and the arctics reproduced northward, those of their seeds lying generally in that direction being the more viable ones under the particular conditions. And both also propagated upward, arriving atop high summits like Dana. In fact, on some lower

whitebark pine at timberline, pruned by wind

a Basque lady

mountains some species must have been "pushed" right off the tops and into oblivion locally by the rising climatic belts, or will be should climatic conditions warm still more and the timberline ascend further.

Climb Mount Dana slowly. Most of it is above timberline, and in the Sierra that means high altitude and accompanying shortness of breath. Dana is so high that it will probably also mean at least a mild dose of mountain sickness — headache, nausea, dizziness, and fatigue in varying degrees.

There is no formal trail as such, but a path that is in places defined by use begins just a short distance east from the Tioga Pass Entrance Station. At the outset, it follows more or less along the park boundary divide or just northeast of it through a lodgepole/whitebark pine stand. The topography here in the pass is hummocky, and the trail swings around ponds and over ridges and crosses meadowed flats that were created by stagnant ice as the last glacier ceased motion, melted, and dropped its load of rock debris. At the edge of one meadow are samples of Basque "ladies" — pinups carved in the thin lodgepole pine bark by shepherds about 1906. Hopefully they did not bring their sheep to here through the park, which did exist then. Perhaps they had fallen victim to an enforcement technique developed by the U.S. Army, then administrator of this and other parks, in its frustration over not getting convictions of trespass grazing violators. The soldiers evicted the sheep on one side of the park and the herders on the other over 40 miles distant. By the time the herders had gotten back to their sheep, the lesson must have been learned.

Continue on toward the slope of Dana, coming closer up under the Lion's Head, and then swing right (southeast) upward, eventually following a natural watercourse up a sloping meadow, climbing above timberline to a tableland above. Do try to stay on the path, for even though not a trail it is easier to follow this than to go cross-country here. Once the route is lost it may be hard to refind, but you can go back to the last known piece if necessary and try again to locate it rather than forge on ahead. Be especially watchful going through dense willows where the trail may be obscured. You can look across these clumps and on up the slope and perhaps see the trail beyond, then head for it by the most open route. It is likely you will come to — or have already come to — rocks with orange patches painted on them to mark the way, but as some of these have rolled downslope over the years they are not always on course. You may also see stacks of rocks, called ducks or cairns, intended to identify the route and often about the only sign of it, but even they are not certain as some indicate side routes.

As you rise, the tree battle appears more severe. The weather here dwarfs the trees, even clipping off flag-like shoots they raise as though to test the climate. Whitebark pines are pressed flat into matted patches

Mt. Dana use trail defined by a rock duck

cairn at edge of upper bench, Mt. Dana beyond, approximate route shown

polemonium, or sky pilot

under the annual snowload and the trees develop into genetic strains that favor clustered, small forms. Growth under such conditions is slow, some trees gaining but an inch in diameter in a century.

Timberline is topped as you rise to a less steep slope in a sort of open bowl. The glacier that flowed through Tioga Pass probably reached only this high, although it likely received some additional ice collected in this depression. Now ascend on the right side of the drainage, heading away from Lion's Head. In this vicinity richly flowered hanging meadows cloak the mountain side, with patches of rocks that actually flow down the slopes over all when the soil is saturated with water and frost. (Note how the earth below some of these rock tongues is pushed into a ridge.) Rock rabbits or pikas (also called conies) are sometimes seen gathering grasses here for their winter "hay". If you don't see them, you may still hear their squeaking (not to be confused with the warning whistle of the marmot, or "rockchuck"). You will probably by now also have seen the Clark's nutcracker, a moderately-large gray and black-and-white bird much like a jay, with a big bill it uses to feed on the nuts of whitebark pine cones, an abundant food just below here.

At the head of the bowl, you arrive at a sort of bench on the mountain. From this spot the summit stands above in plain view. The altitude here is 11,600 feet, while Dana's top is at 13,053 feet, 1.1 miles away. There may be a big rock cairn here. Note this or something else distinctive here to sight on for when you return so you can relocate the route you have followed so far, which will be out of sight from above. Now head to the left for the lower notch on the left shoulder of Dana, skirting up about the edge of the concavity on the side of the mountain slope directly in front. From the notch, follow the near side of the ridge, heading right, all the way up to the summit. The use path shows here and there, plus cairns and patches of orange paint on the rocks. Close to the summit, the rocks will move underfoot, tilting and sometimes throwing you off balance. Be prepared for some quick footwork. And also be careful not to dislodge anything that could roll on persons below you. Call "Rock!" if you fail.

The area of the summit and the bench that grades into the upper slopes is a felsenmerre, or sea of rock. These are common at high altitudes where frost is frequent but where there have not been glaciers to remove the rubble generated by the freezing and thawing action. Plant growth and chemical action in the cold is too slow to allow much soil to form, and what does is blown away. The rounded topography here is as old as the summit of Half Dome, some 10 million years. In fact, in the drainage just south from here, between Mount Dana and Mount Gibbs, stream gravels from this pre-glacial period can still be observed. As you rise along the summit ridge, similar surfaces are seen to the east on the Dana Plateau across Glacier Canyon and to the north in the vicinity of Lee Vining Peak, Saddlebag Lake, Mount Conness, and Shepherd Crest. A person with some imagination can in their mind's

Four views east to south from summit Mt. Dana
1) Mono Lake over Dana Plateau

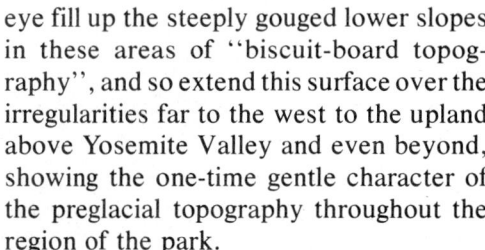

2) Mono Craters

eye fill up the steeply gouged lower slopes in these areas of "biscuit-board topography", and so extend this surface over the irregularities far to the west to the upland above Yosemite Valley and even beyond, showing the one-time gentle character of the preglacial topography throughout the region of the park.

The top of Mount Dana is 13,053 feet above sea level, in Yosemite second only to Mount Lyell, which itself is seen to the south far up the Lyell Canyon of the Tuolumne River on the horizon, above its glacier. The near peak, just south of us and reddish like Dana, is Mount Gibbs. Under our summit to the east is Dana Glacier, in Glacier Canyon, best seen by walking south then east on down the Dana Ridge. The wild Dana Lake below the glacier is often colored pale green with glacial flour. An ice tongue reaches up here from the glacier — but don't try to descend it without experience and equipment — a cornice may overhang the top, a bergschrund crevasse may block the final passage onto the glacier far below, and the glacier itself is extremely steep and often its ice is too firm to make steps.

Over the canyon holding Dana Glacier is Dana Plateau, a rolling pre-glacial erosion surface already noted. Beyond, lying in the treeless desert is Mono Lake, left from the last glacial period and without present outlet, thus shrinking in size and consequently gaining in salt content as the water evaporates from its surface. Pale-gray barely-extinct volcanoes stand south of the lake's right shore, and although the highest of them rises nearly 2,000 feet, we look down on them. In the center of the lake are volcanic islands, by their colors giving clues as to where the lake has stood since they formed (the light colors indicating salt deposits on the otherwise dark volcanic rocks). Behind all stand the White Mountains.

To the north is Mount Conness, along the main ridge of the Sierra. To the west is Tuolumne Meadows, and left of that and closer are the multiple cirques of Kuna Crest, at least one carrying a rock glacier. Over 20 full-sized lakes are in view.

You may also meet one of the successive generations of Oscars here, hungry marmots all, or see their signs. They are usually near the summit register, the most popular lunch spot.

Enjoy, too, the tiny alpine wildflowers, especially the traditional flower of the High Sierra mountaineer — the sky pilot, or polemonium. But don't pick one for your hat or hair; the days when that was tolerable are over, for there are now more people than polemoniums, and these blue-petaled

Dana Meadows and Tuolumne Meadows from summit Mt. Dana

3) Kuna Glacier

4) Mt. Lyell above its glaciers ↑

flowers with their hairy and sticky leaves to protect them from moisture loss in the high altitude can only grow here in the zone above 12,000 feet, where there aren't many acres. Some plants in this "land above the trees" form mats like pin cushions, and virtually all are perennials to overcome the hazard of failing to propagate in any one year. There are several kinds of lichens on the otherwise bare rock surfaces, including one of chartreuse color and an orange one that looks like the paint marks we have been following but might lead you to unwanted discoveries.

Return by the same route, perhaps with a wander about the leveler plateau area below the main summit, and then back to the use trail at its edge, keeping your eye on the cairn there or other landmark you previously selected. In flatter areas where there is sand, watch for grains of frothy pumice rock, blown here during some recent eruptions of the volcanoes you just saw east of Mount Dana. Light, some pieces even float on water. Try one below some snowbank or in a rivulet pool.

Winter and spring ascents can be made by ski mountaineers, following the general topographic clues given here, as all ground-trail signs will be covered. If the snow surface is hard, metal ski edges may be needed, or boot crampons. The last 400 feet of the summit is often open rock even in winters when most other areas here are snowy.

marmot, Oscar?

Map of Tioga Pass-Mt. Dana

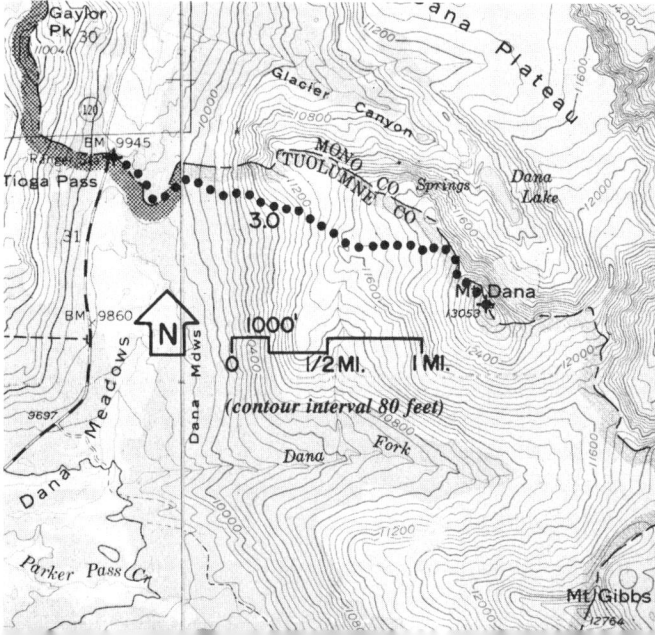

9) LIVING GLACIERS
Lyell and Maclure

Start and Finish: Tuolumne Meadows at Dog Lake/Pacific Crest-John Muir Trails parking area (8,700 feet)

	Elevation gain, feet	Elevation loss, feet	Distance miles	Time hours
One-way Tuolumne Meadows to Lower Base Camp (9,000 feet)	400	0	8.7	5
One-way Tuolumne Meadows to top of Mount Lyell (13,114 feet)	4,114	0	13.5	13
One-way return from top of Mount Lyell	0	4,414	13.5	8
Round-trip totals:	4,414	4,414	27.0	3 days

Seasons: summer and fall

Note: rock and glacier climbing skills and equipment required for summit.

Map: page 71

Mt. Lyell, Mt. Maclure, and glaciers

To understand how Yosemite fits together — whether one be a botanist, landscape artist, hiking enthusiast, geologist, or other soul curious by avocation or by vocation — one has to understand its glaciers. Yosemite has two kinds — living and past. It is the glaciers of the past, extensive ice streams up to 60 miles long and 5,000 feet deep, that shaped the scene we see today and that determined where plants would live, how canyons would turn, and where a trail ascent would top out. Yet it is the living glaciers that give the insight to realize what happened in Yosemite, and just how.

The park has several living glaciers along its eastern Sierra crest and others are just over the boundary nestled under park peaks such as Conness, Dana, and Kuna. The two largest are inside the park, however. These are Lyell Glacier (actually two separate ice bodies now) and adjacent Maclure Glacier. Although so small as to be not recognized as glaciers by some early observers, a trip to these reveals the mechanics of glacier flow — with crevassing, headwall sapping, depositing of moraine rubble at sides and snouts, and the washing out of ground-up rock as glacial flour in discharge streams. Besides, it's a fine mountain adventure. Or maybe that's the main reason to go.

breaking through an ice-bridge

Glaciers do not form everywhere or all the time. They do form where or when more snow falls than melts over a period of years, the snow metamorphosing into ice in the lower layers as it accumulates in depth and as pressure at the bottom thus increases from the overburden. This may occur because of a heavy winter snowfall, a cloudy and cool summer, or both. Naturally, accumulation of snow is more likely to occur if there is shade, as on the northeast side of a tall peak which blocks out all or part of the sun during the warmer parts of the days. Occasionally in recent years there have been intermittent periods of glacier growth. Generally, however, they have shrunk since their advance in the mid-19th century when they were nearly twice as large as now and pushing actively against their terminal moraines at the ends of their snouts. At the same general time, Alaskan glaciers also were advancing, as were those in Europe, one of which buried a church in an Alpine valley!

As a glacier grows in size, it becomes thicker, and when about 200 feet thick, the lower layers begin to flow as a plastic, carrying the upper ones along as a brittle solid. This top zone breaks into crevasses, or tension cracks. These open at the glacier's sides because the ice in the center flows faster than that along the edges where there is friction with the canyon walls, and they also open in the center where the floor under the glacier is irregular. They widen through melting in the summer and are closed again either by continued movement or by winter snows. The uppermost of these crevasses is the bergschrund, formed where the glacier pulls away from its peak, and because it pulls away. The bergschrund crack extends down through the ice to the rock of the peak that spawned its glacier, the line between the bergschrund and the rock marking the "schrundline". Upslope from this line the peak is hackled and steep. Downslope the ground is smoothed and even polished by the flowing ice, which streams down the low parts of the landscape, following and filling stream valleys until the low-altitude climate is warm enough to melt the ice away.

Just this happened when Yosemite Valley was shaped to its present form, for at 4,000 feet, the Valley has always been well below the altitude zone of snow accumulation. It was from peaks like Mount Lyell and Mount Maclure that the ice came, and on several separate occasions. Following the last major ice advance, the glaciers once more melted away completely. Then the present little ice age began, with newly reborn glaciers occupying the same old cirques. The living glaciers at Lyell and Maclure today are left from this more recent period. Will they continue shrinking? Or will they grow again? Regardless, their existence seems to contradict the notion that the Ice Age is over. So does Antarctica.

Mount Lyell is a glacial horn peak, the same type as the Matterhorn of Switzerland. It is eaten into on three sides by glaciers, but with a small sloping summit platform left from before the Ice Age. Today it has glaciers again, and these must be negotiated on most routes to climb to the peak summit. The topmost block itself is a simple rock-climb — simple, but a rock climb, and not a good place to gain experience. Do that closer to the road where help is at hand if needed. A rope is useful for

Mt. Lyell trail is near level the first 9 miles

most people. Some might notice mountain sickness — nausea, fatigue, etc. — near the summit, as it is well above the sea level abodes of most of its climbers, and the thin air takes effect.

Mount Lyell can be climbed from Tuolumne Meadows in one day. Three are recommended, however — one into base camp, one up the peak and perhaps to Maclure Glacier and back to base camp, and one to return. Winter ascents have been made. The first ski ascent was in 1936, with five ski-mountaineers starting from Happy Isles in Yosemite Valley, taking two days for the approach and one glorious day for the final summit ascent, followed on the return by a 7,000 foot downhill run that lasted well into the moonlight.

The trail starts in Tuolumne Meadows. Turn south off the Tioga Road at a point 0.4 mile east of the Tuolumne River bridge. Wilderness permits, which you will need, are issued in the parking area here on the right side of the road. A closer place to park for the Lyell trip is another 0.4 mile up this Old Tioga Road, past the ranger station, at the next parking area, on the left (north) side of the road where the Dog Lake/Sierra Crest-John Muir Trail crosses. Your trail is below this latter parking area, between the road and the river.

Note the trail junction just west of the parking area. From there one trail follows close to the road to the Tuolumne Meadows High Sierra Camp 0.3 mile to the east. Our trail follows closer to the north bank of the Dana Fork of the Tuolumne River, the stream here, heading upriver (east). From this roadside junction, it is 13.5 miles to Mount Lyell. The first 8.7 miles of the trip is up the almost level Lyell Canyon to the Lyell Base Camp at 9,000 feet altitude, only 400 feet higher than here!

Up the trail 300 yards from the start, the trail forks. Take the right branch and cross the Dana Fork on a bridge. One hundred yards past this is another trail junction, the route on the left heading up the right (east) bank of the Dana Fork to Gaylor Lakes (4.3 miles) and Mono Pass (8.4 miles). Our trail stays to the right here, venturing through the lodgepole forest strip of half a mile that here divides the Dana Fork from its sister Lyell Fork, to which we are heading. Cross the bridge over the Lyell Fork and in 0.1 mile more reach another trail, this one coming up from the right along the west bank of the Lyell Fork from the Tuolumne Meadows Campground. Turn left (east), following the signs toward Donohue Pass (although we won't go quite that far).

From here the route is simpler, with fewer intersections and less diverging use trails. Some rerouting has been done to avoid more fragile meadow areas where 6 or 8 parallel tracks were carved in wetter places in past years. Glimpses of the river are seen, and there are large ponds where ducks may be nesting. Spots where avalanches have swept down and carried trees out onto the valley floor are seen, all the trees lying tops out toward the valley center. Later in the summer, after the snow cover is gone off the glacier and ice itself is melting, releasing its contained finely ground rock, milky white glacier flour may be seen in the stream.

There are three base camps to choose from for your camp — Lower, Middle, and Upper. All have water, but the most wood is naturally at Lower Base Camp. Gasstove cooking only is allowed at the Middle and Upper — no wood fires. You can go as far today as you wish; just remember that tomorrow you will have to make up the balance. There is even an Upper Upper Base Camp, but much higher and there aren't even many flat rocks for a bed, let alone anything soft.

The trail up Rafferty Creek to Vogelsang High Sierra Camp exits on the right (west), half a mile after the point where we crossed the Lyell Fork. And 4.2 miles above that trail junction, another trail also turns off to the right, up Ireland Creek to Ireland and Evelyn Lakes. Lower Lyell Base Camp is

3.0 miles from this Ireland Creek junction.

The climb begins at the Lower Base Camp and continues from there, following the right (west) bank of the Lyell Fork. Avalanche tracks with broken trees are passed, coming down from the right above the trail, showing this not to be a completely safe winter route. A view back from a higher point on the trail shows the meander loops of the Lyell Fork at the head of its flat canyon.

At Middle Base Camp, the trail crosses the stream via a trail bridge to its eastern side.

At Upper Base Camp, the trail crosses back to the west again, then ascends an open rocky slope with willows and sparse trees to the Upper Upper Base Camp, a picturesque site with a few whitebark pines just where the trail tops out and crosses a small stream. At the head of the meadow here, the use path to Mount Lyell leaves the John Muir Trail, at a point still about a mile before Donohue Pass. This spot was a chipping site of Indians, and large flakes of their black volcanic arrowhead rock abound in the soil (if your predecessor hikers were as thoughtful as you and left them.)

Now the route stays close to the base of the ridge on the right, well above the canyon floor. A partly worn-in use path with rock ducks (artificially stacked boulders) are the most that mark the way, so navigate by map now, too. At the end of this ridge the basin of Lyell Glacier opens to view, the slope becomes rocky, and the use path gets harder to follow. Head for the westernmost of the two ice lobes that you see, the one that is to the right of the dividing "cleaver" ridge. Ascend to the point in this lobe's moraine that is highest on the slope so that you can walk over solid rock as far as possible. Pick your route carefully to the moraine, as there are excessively steep spots which could delay you.

At the moraine, climb up and over to the other side, taking care not to roll rocks on yourself or your companions below, for even the large boulders are extremely unstable, dumped there helter-skelter by the retreating ice or in some cases consisting only of a veneer of broken rocks over a core of melting ice.

At the edge of the ice, put your crampons on your boots and get your ice axe out. Although you probably won't need either for awhile, they are easier to put on where you can sit, and you can get some practice in their use before you reach the steeper upper ice, where you may soon have need for the experience. The ice axe is used to

Mt. Lyell and Glaciers (East Lobe on left; West Lobe on right); showing approximate route to summit

Mt. Lyell, above West Lobe Lyell Glacier, showing approximate route to summit

chop steps, for balance, and to stop a sliding fall down the glacier by dragging the pick on the ice while held close to the chest, slowly at first, and in such a way as not to be impaled. Avoid slopes steep enough to require such a skill if you currently lack it.

From here on, if not before, is a world of change, with the glacier never the same two months in a row nor from season to season. All summer long it transforms from a robust snow field (that may give comparatively easy access to the peak) to the "bones" of ice that remain in autumn, steep and hard. You must judge the situation for yourself and respond to the mountain, using the directions here only if they seem to fit, modifying them otherwise. ("If in doubt, chicken out" is again a good motto.)

Where snow rather than ice covers parts of the surface, deep pits melted by the sun may make travel difficult. If so, go around these patches if you can. If the glacier surface is hard ice, use extreme caution, possibly stay off it altogether. Usually there are no crevasses in the lower parts of either the West or the East Lobes of Lyell Glacier, but like all true glaciers, there will at least be a bergschrund crevasse up near the headwall. Early in the summer, or all year after heavy winters, the crevasses may still be concealed under bridges built by the last winter's snow, potential traps for mountaineers. Where uncertain, probe with the shaft of your ice axe to see if it pokes through into a covered hole. Also, if anywhere near a crevasse or a suspected crevasse, be roped up with your partners and have a plan worked out in advance for rescue that would work no matter which of you fell in.

Mount Lyell is the block of rock directly above the ice of the West Lobe, its summit on the top left of the block. One route heads directly for this up the glacier and the cliff above it, crossing the bergschrund if feasible and climbing the hackled rock on the opposite side. But another way that is often safer and easier heads to the right toward the saddle on the skyline between Mount Lyell and Mount Maclure. All should go at least to this saddle and look down the cliff there into the headwaters of the Lyell Fork of the Merced River. From this saddle, to ascend Mount Lyell, turn left (southeast) along the ridge that leads along the skyline, bypassing the bergschrund at the head of the glacier by staying on the rock. In this stretch the route is a bona-fide Class 3 mountain climb, requiring route-finding, the use of

Mt. Lyell, showing bergschrund above West Lobe Lyell Glacier, and approximate route to summit

Mt. Lyell summit steep tableland, or felsenmerre

sun pits

your hands, and a rope for confidence as well as safety. Find your general path while still below, noting prominent shapes and memorizing them so you can stay on course when up close, then pick your way up among the granite blocks, slopes, and chimneys, using cracks and ledges where you can. (If the height is too scary for you, find out early and retreat in wisdom, then enjoy exploring the ponds, rocks, and flowers below with the time saved.)

Look back occasionally so you will recognize the route when you return. In a few hundred feet you will pass the steep section and top out on a slope you can walk up. At this point, stop and take careful note of where you are so you do not miss your climbing route when you come back down.

Now walk up to the summit over felsenmerre, rock lying here since before the Ice Age and deeply shattered following eons of action by frost in its joint-cracks. This surface is a portion of one of the original landscapes extant before Yosemite was glaciated. Even now it does not hold much snow in winter, most being swept away by the wind typical of storms here. In August you will see the blue polemonium in bloom, its roots ensconced in the rock crevices holding the little soil that does exist in this environment, growing here in clumps as perennials for year after year, where you can only linger during the warmest part of a summer day.

Atop the summit block, you are as high as you can get in Yosemite without jumping up, and most people won't, because the opposite side of the mountain drops off here in a cliff. To the left (southeast) side is another small glacier, Southeast Lyell Glacier, and beyond to the south stretches the wilderness of the High Sierra, the John Muir Trail winding through it clear to Mount Whitney. The slope of the Sierra can be seen declining to the west, and there again is Yosemite Valley trenched into it, although you will be able to see little more than the back of Half Dome standing on the rim. To the north you can see Lembert Dome in Tuolumne Meadows. Hopefully you will have along a map of the entire park so you can spot the many other landmarks and points, too numerous to list here. Watch, too, for bighorn sheep. You proba-

Getting up to the rocks

Lyell Canyon, looking north from Mt. Lyell summit

Mt. Maclure (at left) from Mt. Lyell summit; route to Maclure Glacier goes through low notch near ridge dividing Maclure and Lyell Glaciers

bly won't see any, for this animal is rare in the Sierra. Yet recent sightings have been reported just to the south of Lyell Glacier. Horns (indicating death of the owner, unlike antlers which are regrown annually) are sometimes found, too.

At the zenith of the Ice Age, ice flowed from this spot away in all directions, filling almost the entire view, with much of it headed for Yosemite Valley. Ice collecting on the mountain's south reached the Valley via the Lyell Fork of the Merced River, and that on the west flowed down Hutchings Creek to join the former stream. The north cirque bowl (where the two glacier lobes are now, reborn in recent time) was the head for the Tuolumne Glacier, and part of that ice even spilled out of Tuolumne Meadows to extend down Tenaya Canyon to Yosemite Valley. And so Mount Lyell is a true glacial horn peak, its three sides eaten into by one glacier each until only a thick horn-like summit block remains.

Start back to camp while there is still ample time, for much or all of the going is cross-country, and you are now more tired and have the more difficult task of climbing down. Besides, there is less light and warmth left in the day, and an accident now would become a rescue in the night.

Walk back down the felsenmerre slope to the steep pitch you climbed, coming to it at the spot you noted earlier, and retrace your route all the way back to camp. It's 13 miles to Tuolumne Meadows.

But if you now have confidence in both your route-finding skill and your ability to cope with the country should you miscalculate, there are more things to do, particularly if you are in good condition and gained the summit earlier in the day.

You can explore more on the West Lobe of Lyell Glacier and go down around the cleaver to the East Lobe and up it to the ridge above where there is a good view of Southeast Lyell Glacier.

From the Lyell-Maclure saddle, you can climb Mount Maclure, although a bit more technical than was Lyell. You can scramble across the steep cleaver ridge separating West Lobe Lyell Glacier from Maclure Glacier through the deepest notch and then drop down onto Maclure's ice (which does have crevasses below its bergschrund and extremely steep ice at its western side). Above this glacier on the right (west) side of Mount Maclure, the rock ridge can be crossed at one point for a good view into Hutchings Creek and a rock glacier there. Pick your route off Maclure Glacier carefully, and then head on down the canyon below around Maclure Lake, staying high on the right (east) side, trending down a long open sloping ridge to the northeast, avoiding the one big cliff by a detour on either side, then dropping into a level lake-dotted basin and through it to the north. Find the more northerly of the outlet streams, then follow the rocky slopes adjacent to its north bank back down to the Upper Upper Base Camp, where you rejoin the John Muir Trail. Be sure to use your map in this route-finding exercise.

If you have now taken all the hikes up to this point in this book, and without mishap,

Clark's nutcracker

you can count yourself a competent summer mountaineer and should be ready to at least begin your own exploring and climbing in the Sierra. With the next trip, to Ostrander Lake or one of its preliminary excursions, you can start learning how to handle yourself in Yosemite in the winter.

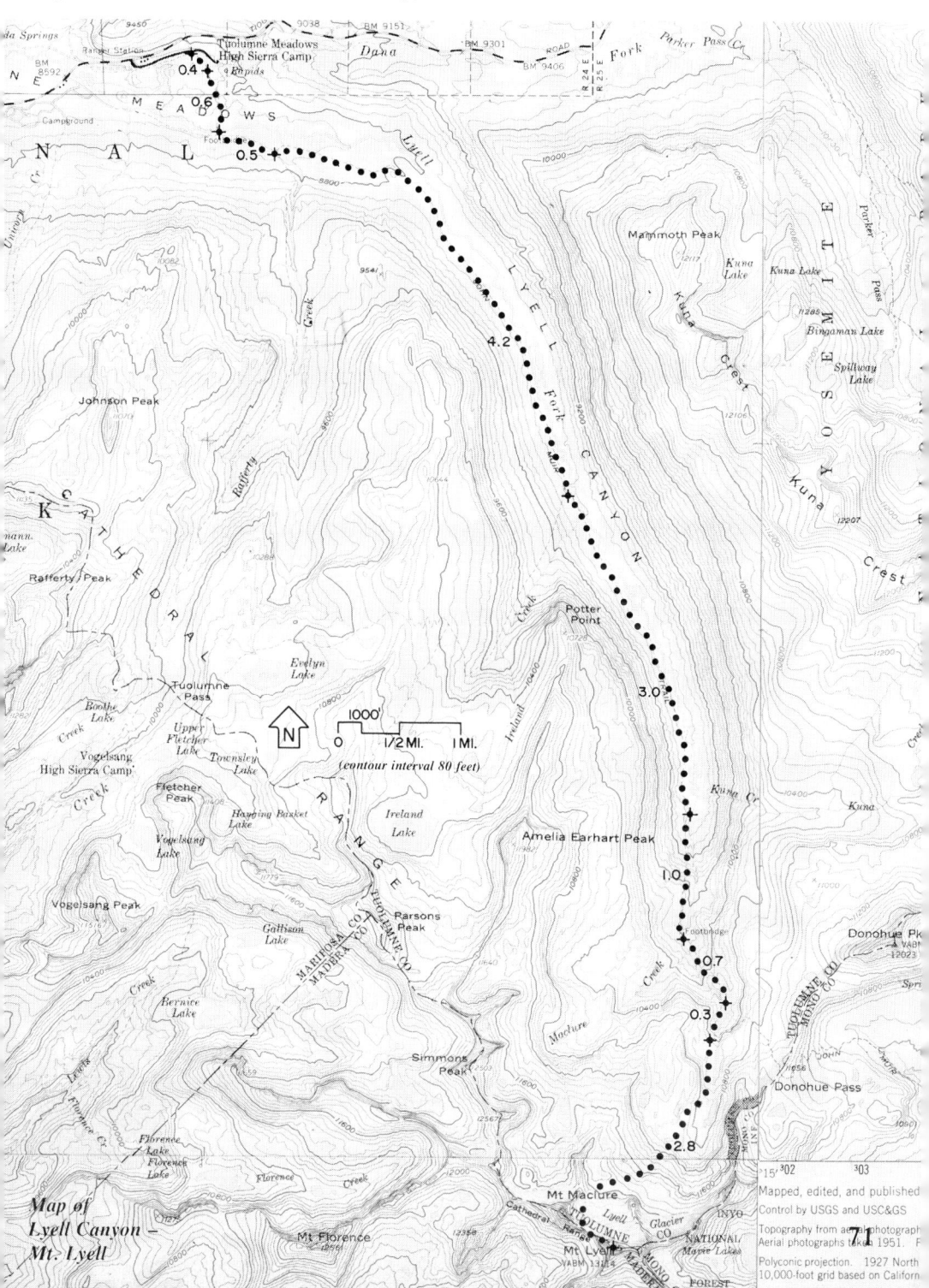

Map of Lyell Canyon – Mt. Lyell

10) *WINTER*
Ostrander Hut Ski Trail

Start and Finish: Badger Pass Ranger Station (7,240 feet)

	Elevation gain, feet	Elevation loss, feet	Distance miles	Time hours
One-way Badger Pass Ranger Station to Ostrander Ski Hut (8,500 feet) via Old Glacier Point Road and Horizon Ridge Trail (#15)	1,960	280	10.0	10
One-way return Ostrander Ski Hut to Badger Pass Ranger Station via Merced Crest Trail (#16)	1,440	2,480	9.9	10
Round-trip totals:	3,400	2,760	19.9	2 days

Seasons: winter and spring; oversnow gear required.

Notes: Full trip requires cross-country skiing or snowshoeing skills. Trip may be shortened if Glacier Point Road is open to Summit Meadows or beyond and parking or shuttle can be arranged, as cars should not be left along road there in case of snowstorm which could close road. Advance reservations are required for use of Ostrander Ski Hut; write to Superintendent, Yosemite National Park, California 95389. Before leaving, check out with ranger at Badger Pass. CHECK IN ON RETURN.

Map: page 77

snow cornice above Ostrander Lake, ski hut on shore

Winter needn't be a time to stop hiking in Yosemite. In fact, as soon as the snow is deep enough to cover the brush and logs and smooth over some of the rocks, new routes open up for cross-country skiing that often make travel easier than in summer. Or you can snowshoe. Yosemite has marvelous over-snow terrain for both.

The first storm of magnitude usually does not hit until November, but often by the end of that month, snow depths are adequate to change from trail boots to ski boots. Snow will continue to accumulate until early May, the snowpack often reaching 10 feet in depth, with about 20 feet the record.

The trips you can make are limited only by your imagination, enthusiasm, and some physical and safety factors, for in winter you travel across a blanket instead of along a line. The Sierra Nevada is mild and clear most days of most winters. But it does earn its name "Snowy Range", and some storms last weeks and dump as much as 10 feet of loose snow (up to 5 feet in a day), leaving backcountry travelers floundering instead of progressing. Avalanches can then rip down mountains, and snowslopes may be unstable for days or weeks. Even skilled mountaineers can be

snow camping

marooned by such conditions, through no fault of their own. There can also be rain in these mountains so near the Pacific Ocean, soaking even a good camp; then it can clear and freeze hard. In spring, especially, there will be streams to cross, often torrents at this season in the warmer afternoons when carrying snowmelt runoff from the heat of the day. Plan, train, and study as you might, you cannot completely avoid these risks; they are inherent in the equation of the Sierra and if you go you accept them whether willingly, knowingly, or otherwise. Few who have not lived in the Sierra understand this. (Where do you live?)

But it is not all gloom and doom — else why would cross-country skiing in the Sierra be growing so in popularity? There are attractions — the scenery is the obvious one, with the peaks and domes taking on new aspects in their white mantles, the waterfalls fringed with white frost dendrites. Most of the geologic features — bedrock granites, glaciers, fracture lines — are covered over; but some — moraine crests, cirque hollows, avalanche chutes, ledges — stand out more clearly at times in winter, emphasized by the snow. The plants are covered, excepting the trees, but year-round residents can be seen in them — mountain chickadees in white firs, red-breasted nuthatches in the red firs, blue grouse, Clark's nutcrackers in the timberline pines, and even the great gray owl especially at Crane Flat and at Bridalveil Creek Meadows on the Glacier Point Road. Woodpeckers are about in variety. The porcupine is in the trees, too, staying high and eating the bark's cambium layer, coming down only when the snow is firm enough to move to a new tall food source. Chickaree squirrels scold from the trees. The longtailed weasel is now the white-furred ermine — a new name to match his new beauty. The long-eared jackrabbit of the meadows turns white, too, like the snowshoe hare does farther north. The coyote remains active in the snow zone, but the mountain lion will probably follow the deer downslope. The bear hibernates, although fitfully, and is apt to come out at warmer times and leave footprints in the snowbanks.

The Ostrander trip is one of the better ones for beginning winter buffs, and is a good one to repeat later, too, for there are many variations to explore. You sign out with a ranger at Badger Pass Ranger Station and follow snow-covered roads or marked oversnow trails.

If this is your very first trip in winter, you should not attempt to reach Ostrander Lake. Instead, take only a portion of the route described, testing your equipment and endurance. Although there is a ski hut at the lake, you might have to know how to survive a Sierra winter night — or several — if you don't make it that far. Also, the hut may be full. Advance reservations are needed to stay there. Make them with

snow monks

touring tracks

Superintendent, Yosemite National Park, California 95389. Bunks, cooking stoves, firewood, and toilets are usually available (check these details), but you must bring your own food and sleeping gear, etc. Some carry a tent just in case.

There are three routes to choose from. Here, we will direct you out one and back on another, these two having more open terrain and hence providing better views and easier route finding.

At Badger Pass, find where the Old Glacier Point Road leaves the parking area (uphill beyond the right side — east — of the ranger station). It will be covered with snow, a narrow slot through the trees. Prepare your skis for an uphill start, then ascend the road through the red fir forest, passing an adjacent aspen grove in a meadow at one spot, to the summit. This is the "true" Badger Pass — high point on the Old Glacier Point Road between the Grouse Creek and Bridalveil Creek drainages. The open slope on the right (south) of the pass is "Old Badger"; it had a rope tow in the early 1930s, operating until the ski area was moved to its location of today.

Now it's downhill, still on the Old Glacier Point Road. In 0.2 mile a snow course is passed, where rangers survey snowdepths and water contents to forecast the Sierra's spring runoff. At 2.2 miles from our start, note the Limit Trail (#13), so-called because it limits how far east lost skiers from Badger Pass might get, leading them back. The new Glacier Point Road, for instance, is half a mile north on this limit trail. In 0.5 mile more, still on the Old Glacier Point Road, arrive at Bridalveil Creek Campground, mainly buried and concealed at this time of year. Here turn left — north — along the campground access road leading in 0.5 mile to its intersection with the new Glacier Point Road, also probably snow-covered here. If the access road is hard to find, merely head cross-country to the north through the open meadows to the new Glacier Point Road. This wide road is a clearly defined swath through the trees, elevated somewhat in places of fills and depressed below shallow banks in places of cuts. This is hard to miss unless the visibility is obscured in a snowstorm or the like, but be sure you don't miss it as the cliffs of Yosemite Valley lie a distance beyond.

(Alternatively to arriving at this spot by the Old Glacier Point Road, you may drive out the present Glacier Point Road — if plowed — to wherever it is closed. Usually you can reach Summit Meadows, 1.5 miles east of Badger Pass, to begin your snow trip there. The problem is that if you stay out overnight and it snows, your car could be marooned there as that is not always plowed out. Perhaps you can arrange a car shuttle or be dropped off. From there follow the unplowed Glacier Point Road to this same junction with the road to Bridalveil Creek Campground.)

Horizon Ridge Trail marker

At the junction of the new Glacier Point Road with the Bridalveil Creek Campground Road, turn right (east) on the new Glacier Point Road. Follow it over the Bridalveil Creek bridge (0.5 mile from here), then go on 0.9 mile more around the road as it bends north and then south to where the Bridalveil Creek Snow Trail exits on the right (south). It may or may not be signed at the road junction. This Bridalveil Creek Snow Trail is marked with bright metal tabs nailed to tree trunks. It goes up through the woods and sparsely forested meadows of the Bridalveil Creek basin to Horizon Ridge, the destination on our route, too. You may take this alternate Bridalveil Creek Snow Trail now, if you wish or on the return. The route described in this book, however, stays higher, giving better views.

There is also a Ghost Forest Loop (Trail 19) going up Bridalveil Creek itself. This loop connector is 3.0 miles long between the Glacier Point Road and where it joins the Bridalveil Creek Trail.

Continue on the new Glacier Point Road, ascending gradually on a generally straight stretch to the start of a curve of the road to the left (north), at a point 0.3 mile from the Bridalveil Creek Snow Trail. This is a vital point that you must find, as here you turn off the wide new Glacier Point Road onto a narrow oversnow trail through the woods. The turnoff is 3.4 miles from the Summit Meadows gate, or 1.7 miles from the Bridalveil Creek Campground road. Find the start of the marked trail on the right (south) side of the road. A sign should be on a treetrunk at the roadside and others in sight beyond, indicating Horizon Ridge Trail (#15). Ostrander Lake and the Ski Hut on its shore are 4.6 miles ahead. The trail leaves the road upward on a fairly steep hillside, heading through the forest.

At the top of the first rise, the trail levels and continues on through alternating open and wooded sections of conifers without much climbing for the next 1.9 miles. Here begin an ascent to the Horizon Ridge dome, cut into on the east by a small ancient glacier. Views of Half Dome, Illilouette Valley, and Horse Ridge open. (Use caution here in snowstorm or fog as the trail comes near the dropoff.) From the dome's top there is an 0.7 mile downhill run to a saddle. Make your turns carefully in case you encounter a tricky snowcrust condition on this south slope. At the saddle the Bridalveil Creek Snow Trail, which we rejected earlier, now joins our route from the right (west). Avoiding it, but continuing

Ostrander Lake

on the Horizon Ridge Trail (#15) toward Ostrander Lake (2.0 miles away), a climb begins up a slope with scattered tall trees, leading past a snow course. Then the trail enters the forest, turning right and upward to begin a dogleg around a hill. (A steeper but shorter alternate may be taken following the summer trail, also marked with oversnow signs.) At the top of the climb, the Ostrander Lake basin is seen below the cliff face of Horse Ridge, an ancient glacial cirque. The lake itself is a white snow-covered flat. It is downhill to the Ski Hut, on the near shore of the lake. If you plan on camping, avoid the lake's outlet, the chilliest spot at night, as the cold dense air will drain through that low place in the topography.

Water is taken from the lake. Use caution around the shore if the ice is thin or if the snow covering it is soft as in warm weather. Probe a ski pole down to check the condition before beginning to cross the lake, and then recheck occasionally.

Around the hut you may see pine martens. At least watch for their tracks in the snow.

The mountain slope across the lake from the ski hut is a good one to ski at times, but watch for crusted snow in the morning after warm days and cold nights. Avalanching is frequent on its right (north) side and anywhere under a large cornice snow overhang.

If you have allowed for an extra day or more, and you are an advanced skier, you might be able to climb Horse Ridge and ski off it back to the lake and hut. Start by going southwest on the Merced Crest Trail (#16) 0.7 mile, first uphill, then level, through a zone of potential avalanche. (This route skirts the north face of Horse Ridge by going around its right – west – end.) Here, the Horse Ridge Trail (#17) exits on the left, uphill. Climbing, a high point of Horse Ridge is reached in about a mile. If not badly corniced with a snow overhang or otherwise hazardous, you can ski off with reasonable safety if you're an advanced skier, and take a long traverse to the left, staying high and heading northwest, descending to the lake, with the chance even for a few turns.

Before going back, however (if early) consider a trip to Buena Vista Peak: You can stay on Trail #17 beyond the top of Horse Ridge and drop down the ridge's backslope 0.7 mile into the saddle dividing the heads of Chilnualna Creek and Buena Vista Creeks. Summer trails along these two creeks cross at this pass, but even their blazes (axe marks on the tree trunks) may not be visible if the snow is more than a few feet deep. Trail #17 ends here. Continue only if you are experienced at finding your own way and at ski mountaineering, for beyond there are increasingly severe avalanche hazards and steep slopes you could slide down in case of a fall. Ascend Buena Vista Peak by first passing right or south around its western side, climbing steeply while doing so, to the back (southwest) slope. From the summit (9,709 feet), descend the northeast ridge to where safe from cornices or other problems and ski off into the side of the bowl above Buena Vista Lake, traversing left and back to the pass or saddle where you began climbing the peak. Then return to the marked Horse Ridge Trail (#17) and climb Horse Ridge, returning to the Ski Hut either down the face or continuing on Trails #16 and #17.

On the way back to Badger Pass from Ostrander Lake, you can retrace your earlier steps and slides, take the alternate Bridalveil Creek Snow Trail or follow a new route along the Merced Crest, the route described here.

Begin this Merced Crest Trail (#16) the same as the trail to the top of Horse Ridge, passing the junction of the Horse Ridge Trail (#17) in 0.7 mile from the Ski Hut. First inspect this stretch from its edge, and if there has been a recent heavy snowfall or the slope otherwise appears or is suspected of being unstable, avoid it and take one of the other routes back. The Merced Crest Trail (#16) holds an undulating course along a slope that is sometimes open and sometimes forested, sometimes steep and sometimes gentle. At 3.6 miles from the Horse Ridge Trail (#17) junction, our trail (#16) dips into a tributary of the Bridalveil Creek valley.

After another 2.4 miles, with as much as 600 feet of elevation gain, the trail drops next into a saddle on the ridgecrest. This is the pass between the heads of Alder Creek and Westfall Meadows. The Limit Trail (#13) extends north from here to the Old Glacier Point Road (our route in) and to the new Glacier Point Road 0.5 mile beyond that. The Limit Trail is a pleasant alternate to our route back to Badger Pass. Our Merced Crest Trail (#16) now climbs and then drops, until circling south around to the west side of Tempo Dome (named for an early ski turn executed on its slopes when a lift was nearby) and then ascending the gentle slope to the top of the main ski

Map of Winter Trails–Badger Pass-Ostrander

(contour interval 80 feet)

on the trail

lift at Badger Pass Ski Area. Return to the base and your car parked at the ranger station by skiing to the right along the gentler trails, where your pack and cross-country ski gear will be more stable even though a curiosity to the snowbunnies on the downhill slopes. Don't neglect to sign in with the ranger.

Congratulations! You are now a Yosemite mountaineer — both summer and winter. Next: El Capitan wall in a blizzard? But that is the subject of another book.

by Robert Barbee